Understanding Addiction:
Behind the Scenes

Sadie Petersen

RoseDog Books

PITTSBURGH, PENNSYLVANIA 15238

RoseDog Books
585 Alpha Drive
Suite 103
Pittsburgh, PA 15238
Visit our website at www.rosedogbookstore.com

ISBN: 978-1-4809-8199-7
eISBN: 978-1-4809-8222-2

About the Author:

Sadie Petersen has dedicated the majority of her life to helping people of all diverse backgrounds. She is a recovery coach, writer, and entrepreneur who is working towards getting her masters certificate in addictions counseling at Portland State University. Sadie spends a great deal of her time working on her non profit called More Than an Athlete, an organization that focuses on giving athletes of all ages a new voice on and off the field by encouraging, empowering, and giving them the tools to be more successful during AND after their sports careers.

Sadie spent a year of her life working as a cocktail server in Las Vegas, where the idea of her experiment, and courage to write this book first came to mind. She has over come major adversity most of her life, with all odds stacked against her, and has proven that you can be anything you want to be with hard work and dedication, and by learning to open your mind to new perspectives. She took on a challenge that has never been heard of, and turned her own circumstances into triumph. She is a master of her fate, and plans to write many more books in the future.

Table of Contents

Acknowledgments

I have so many people to thank who have helped to inspire me to write this book:

To ALL the brave people who allowed me to ask them personal questions about their own stories, I am so grateful for your strength and honesty.

To my family, especially my mom and grandma for believing in me and supporting me through everything.

To my friends, who didn't laugh when I told them my dreams and visions about this book.

To Chandler, and Dominique, for proving that you can win the war against addiction.

To Roston, for listening to me read the same chapters to him over and over, while also putting up with my crazy mood swings in the process.

Dedication

I have dedicated this book to the memory of my friend Zach
Tackwell, whose music and courage to be different inspired
me to find my truth, and to write this book. I have also dedicated this book to all the people who have friends and family
members that struggle with addiction, to my loved ones who
struggle with addiction, and to those who have beat it. And
last, to my Poppa, for stepping in as a father figure to every
one of my family members, and for filling a huge void in my
life as a young woman.

Chapter 1: It's Time

Let me just start by saying congratulations. For what right? Well, there's a reason you picked up this book, and now you have officially taken your first step to gaining control back over your life. It's finally time. It's time to make a change in your OWN journey. You've exhausted all of your options with your loved ones addiction, and now you are either looking for answers on how to get through it, trying to learn more about addiction to try and help them, or, you just really like to read and learn new subjects, either way, I'm just glad you chose my book.

Unfortunately, those who have decided to start reading my book have most likely faced some pretty unpleasant days that they won't ever get back. Painfully, most of us who have loved ones with an addiction problem have been fighting this battle with them for way to long, producing little, to no results in the process of recovery. Because there are no REAL and permanent answers on how to better understand and cope with your love ones addiction problem, trial and error, long stressful nights, and an abundance of broken promises has probably become a vicious pattern with in your home for years.

The majority of parents and friends who have a loved one with an addiction, often share a similar mentality in regards to not understanding WHY this is happening to someone they love. And, because most people think they are capable of fixing every problem themselves and refuse to change their own habits, they continue to be disappointed and let down by their loved ones day after day.

Without useful coping mechanisms from both the user and their loved one with in this fight, this style of living often results in a chaotic, misunderstood, whirlwind of never ending pain and suffering, with continuous strain on everyone involved. I think that anyone reading this book can all agree on that. But, thankfully, it doesn't have to be this way anymore!!

If you are someone who has a loved one suffering from addiction, than most likely you have found yourself tangled deep into a cycle that you can't seem to climb your way out of. Unfortunately, this is all to common lately. You probably find yourself crying at least twice a week, you constantly are being told by others to let go, persistently asking yourself what you did wrong as a mother, continuously being questioned for why you continue to enable your child, and, most likely have been told the same advice over and over again, as if you didn't already know that what you are doing to try and help your loved one, probably is not very effective. Sound anything like you?

Now let me guess, at the end of the day, when it all comes down to it, your initial response to all of this backlash you get from other people is usually always the same thing right – "well he is my child or he is my (whatever they are to you), and I will never turn my back on him." Am I right?

One year has went by, two years, and now it's been five. Five LONG, stressful years full of anxiety and pain because "he is my child and I'll never turn my back on him" was so consistent and easy to say, that it became your only answer.

Now, It's been five years and still, nothing has changed. You have found yourself buried so deep in a financial hole because for years you did NOTHING to really help your situation, and instead, continued to always give him or her money and a place to stay, OR, said you were going to cut him off, but never really did because you didn't want him dying on the streets. Still sounding anything like your situation?

Well, let me ask you something – how's that situation working out for you? You already know that answer, so I won't for you.

If you're anything like me, you absolutely hate being told the same advice on something that you already know the answer to, so instead of having to hear the same thing multiple times and wanting to punch everyone in the room for repeating it, you simply fix the problem head on and explain to them what you did differently this time to create a positive result. On the other hand, if you're anything like my family, which I hope you're not, you hear good advice that you KNOW can help you make a difference for the better, but, instead of trying to find a solution and fix the problem right then, you still continue to do the same thing repeatedly, in hopes for a different response the next time. Welp, guess what, that's the definition of insanity. So, let's stop doing that starting TODAY.

This book isn't going to be that nagging uncle telling you to kick your son out on the streets, it's not going to tell you what you should and shouldn't do about your sister, grandson, daughter, mom, brother or best friends' addiction, either. I'm also not going to hammer you with statistics and big words about addiction that make no sense, or stuff a bunch of scientific jargon down your throat. What I am going to provide you with is some REAL personal shit about my own life, some real stories, some real struggles addicts might be afraid to tell you themselves, and some REAL advice and "answers," by giving you a look behind the scenes of drug addiction. This book is about helping you, and so many others like you, to take a deeper look inside addiction, to help you understand this lifestyle on a more extensive level, and to help you find the peace and understanding you might be searching for. It is my goal that after reading my book, every reader will leave with the ability to think objectively and critically about the severity that comes with addiction, and will learn to apply their own behaviors in situations that may arise with their loved ones addiction from here on out. My hope is that after reading my book, my audience WILL understand this lifestyle more clearly and be able to apply it to their own lives to create improved outcomes for the long run.

Every one of you have probably rummaged through the internet far and wide for information about how to understand an addicts' mind. But, no matter how many times you read something, if you don't understand the concept of how it functions, the words become a foreign language to you, just like with anything you've never really experienced yourself. Facts, statistics, doctors' advice, and science can only take an outsider's perspective on an addicts mind so far. Professionals on this topic only provide their audience on how someone's body reacts to a drug physically and mentally by using statistics and scientific language that make it difficult for people to fully comprehend what the F is really going on, and WHY it's happening. This isn't enough to help someone understand how drugs actually make your body FEEL and how your mind reacts to them, often because professionals on this topic don't use real life scenarios, just a bunch of big words they made up in a science lab. Without actually experiencing something yourself, your ideas on the subject, and your ability to fully understand something will always be misrepresented. For example, a surgeon doesn't just become a surgeon by only reading and researching their practice. A surgeon becomes a surgeon by learning and understanding how the body functions through real hands on situations, and by actually performing their practice on the patients who need their help, thus, becoming an expert in their field through REAL hands on experiences. The point I'm trying to make here is that until you really experience something yourself, you will always have just words, descriptions, others' advice, and your own basic knowledge on the subject that you heard or read somewhere. Sometimes this just isn't enough, and I'm here to help you see and feel the difference. Below, I will be providing you with some essential education that I've read about in articles to show you how others portray this lifestyle, vs. what I can help you understand about this lifestyle using a different perspective.

Prepare yourself, the next little section can get kind or boring and repetitive. So, if you want to skip it, please be my guest because I'm pretty sure you already know, and have read all this shit somewhere else. I promise, the next chapters will get into the good stuff, I just want you to see the difference of what the internet can provide you with, vs. what I can provide you with, that will help readjust your actions and outlook on addiction to gain your own life back.

Addiction is described as a chronic disease characterized by drug seeking, and for most users is described as compulsive, or difficult to control. Over time, drug use causes the brain to change, which then challenges an addicted person's self-control, making it hard to resist intense urges that the drugs bring. When an addict is rewarded with whatever drug of choices' "high" they are seeking, their body begins to remember this feeling, creating a circuit change, causing their body and mind to crave and think it needs more, thus, the continued use for more pleasure.

Over a period of time, an addicts brain adjusts to the excess dopamine it has received, which in turn eventually begins to reduce the high that the person first felt during their initial use. After continued use, their body builds up a tolerance, causing the user to take more of the drug, in hopes to receive the same high as before. This creates different stages of dependency within the cycle of drug abuse.

There are many different factors that play into becoming an addict. Drugs do not discriminate based on socioeconomic status, gender, or race. Genetics, development and environment can influence the risk for addiction, but not one single factor is the sole person for the reason behind someone's addiction.

As a person continues to use drugs, the brain adjusts to the excess dopamine by making less of it and reducing the ability of cells in the reward circuit to respond to it. In return, an addict then might take more of the drug, and as I mentioned above, this is to try and achieve the same high as the original high they once felt. When your body craves one thing, such as drugs, it can then cause other forms of pleasure someone once enjoyed to become less pleasurable - like food, sex or social activities, and, can even take certain feelings away because the brain and nerves have began to rely on that one substance. Long term use can affect someones' memory, behavior and ability to cope with real situations, and slowly takes away the ability of the brain to function normally without it.

Once someone takes drugs, their brain compulsively continues to seek out these substances regardless of negative consequences. The changes that happen in their brain alter its structure and function, and over time an addict's self-control and decision-making abilities become greatly distorted by the drug.

The majority of drugs including opioids impact dopamine which regulates everything from motivation to emotion. Ultimately, the effects of the drugs lead to harmful behaviors and negative thought processes that the person had before they began using drugs. Drugs can completely change the structure of someone's mind in a short matter of time. Like other diseases that affect the mind and body, drug addiction is progressive.

As I sit here and re-read what I just wrote, I literally gained nothing from it and hate that this is seriously the only kind of information out there about the effects of drugs on humans. I feel like I was writing the same thing over and over, and none of it has ever actually helped me UNDERSTAND addiction. Sadly, this is the only kind of information online, that I remember learning about in school, and in books that I could find about addiction, and frankly, it was pretty boring to read about. I promise that is over with now, so just keep reading!

Now that I have supplied you with some "necessary" knowledge on how addiction is formed, and all the other boring statistics provided by doctors and health care professionals, now I will help you understand what you will "never understand." Through out the next few chapters, I am going to be breaking down some of the material I mentioned above through a brighter and more in depth lens, by providing you with real information and stories from myself, current addicts, those who have beaten addiction, and by mothers, brothers, fathers and friends who have a loved one who uses drugs. Let me present you with the REAL truth behind drug addiction. Let me help you change your life for good.

Chapter 2: I'll Just Never Understand

Time and time again you find yourself asking the same questions. How can he not love his child? How can he do to his child, what his father did to him? How can she choose this life over her family? What did I do wrong as a parent? Is this my fault? Why would someone want to live this kind of lifestyle? "I'll just never understand."

So, how can I help you truly understand the life of an addict. Well, I can't. But, what I can do is give you a different perspective on this lifestyle, and give a you a deeper look inside why they do what they do, to aid you and your loved ones by giving you the techniques you need to help cope and understand addiction through a more stress free, and caring way.

First thing you need to understand is that the majority of all families have one thing in common, their family is not perfect. Studies show that almost every single family has an addict of some sort with in their immediate family, and 1 out of every 4 families have a family member who struggles with drug addiction. So, the feeling of isolation you feel, take a deep breath because you are not alone in this. Families of all classes hide their families addictions, due to embarrassment, shame, hopelessness, feeling lost, and feeling like nothing will ever change. All these feelings and emotions you have felt, someone else who is close to you, a neighbor, or even a friend has probably experienced at one point in their lives as well. This is becoming more and more normal, and I am here to help you get through this!

Here's the second important message you need to come to terms with. IT IS NOT YOUR FAULT. Whether you are an addict now, your child saw this lifestyle while growing up, you weren't there for your child during their adolescent stage; OR maybe you were even the best parent in the world, one vital note you need to remember is the fact that an addict becomes an addict, on their own. Yes, you or other outside factors - such as being born into a family of addicts, or experiencing different traumas that made them more susceptible to the lifestyle, may have played a part in the addicts choice to initially use the drug, but, your loved ones decisions throughout their lives, are made completely on their own. PEOPLE become addicts because they have not learned how to cope with their traumas, thus, they blame their faults and decisions on others, instead of taking control of their own lives, and changing their habits. Faults and responsibility are two things that a lot of people get confused with. Yes, it might have been someone else's fault that your son or daughter saw drugs growing up, or that the doctor prescribed your child pain pills after a surgery, but fault cannot be confused with responsibility, because every single person has the ability to choose to do something, or to decline it. If someone chooses to do drugs, that is THEIR fault, and then becomes THEIR responsibility to change their behavior. NOT yours. When you as an outsider can learn to understand an addict on a different level, and learn that addiction is extremely complicated, you're better equipped to help that person, and better yet, help yourself cope with it as well. Here's how I can help you understand this lifestyle from a look on the inside.

To begin, let me help by giving you logic pertaining to some of the questions you ask yourself everyday, and give you answers behind the famous saying "I will just never understand." One question I hear the most from loved ones of an addict is "how can he not love his own child, and how can he do to his child, what his father or mother did to him?" Well, before I answer that, one important step you need to take when these types of questions arrive, is learning to answer questions with more logic (finding solutions that actually make sense) so that your thought process in these situations become more stable each time questions like this arise.

For example, because I gave myself real time to understand this question when I was asked the first time, I was able to answer it more rationally.

The answer to the question above became more clear and simple for me with real thought, because I knew I needed to be more levelheaded while thinking about it. So, instead of taking everything personal, I took a few deep breaths before I blurted out my answer, and instead, gave myself real time to answer LOGICALLY.

Now, before you ask yourself that question again "how can he not love his child, or how can he abandon his child," I want you to take five minutes to yourself first to try and come up with two logical explanations to this question, to help you answer your own question. Write your answer below:

1.

2.

I hope that went well for you! If you couldn't come up with anything, that's okay. This is why I'm here to help guide you in the right direction.

First and foremost, if a user has a child during the time of his or her drug use, it most likely was not supposed to be apart of their lifestyle. So, when a child is born from an act that was never supposed to originally happen, during a time when an addict is still using, why would you expect them to all of a sudden change their current behaviors? They didn't for you, or for themselves, so why would they for someone else? You have to start putting logic into play when dealing with addiction, or you will continue to be bitter and angry towards your loved one without true understanding, and continue to be left with false hope and unanswered questions.

Secondly, how can you expect someone to know how to be a good or a present parent, if they didn't have one themselves! When you lack education and guidance from a mother or father, your upbringing looks a lot different than those who are privileged enough to have both parents involved. You lack love, feelings of emptiness reside, and you often lose the ability to feel and see things others are fortunate enough to have. When a user lacks the love from a missing parent in their own lives, they often lose the ability to feel certain things for people no matter how hard they try because they had to learn to block this part of them for so long. So, before assuming that they just don't want to be apart of their child's life, try putting yourself in their shoes for once, not everyone is you, and not everyone deals with things the same way.

Now you're probably thinking, well a human life should be able to stop them from doing what they are doing. Again, sadly, that's hardly ever the case. Addiction is drug driven, NOT family or love driven. Especially for a man. An addict does what they need to do to survive and get their next high, taking care of themselves is hard enough, they aren't focused on what they brought into this world. Not being able to take care of their own child just becomes another reason for them to get high.

Don't get me wrong, this doesn't always necessarily mean that the user doesn't love or want to be apart of their child's life, but, most often they are ill prepared for a child, and their conscience of what is right and wrong no longer exists, thus, a child to them is just something that gets in their way of using, and usually they can't afford to do both, drugs usually become the winner.

To further this statement with more reasoning behind it, in some cases, a user knows what they are doing isn't right, and as a result, they remove themselves out of the situation completely so their son or daughter doesn't have to experience that lifestyle, or see them the way they are.

In some cases, the only way an addict knows how to connect with someone is by using with someone, often being their own child, so they begin using together as a form of bonding. This coping mechanism then forms a vicious cycle of a user thinking they can only be loved by someone else who is a user also, someone who they think "understands them," and creates a circle of acceptance between the two.

Anyway, as you can see, there are many different reasons that play apart in why an addict abandons their child, as the sober one, the only thing you have control over is taking responsibility with in yourself to not get caught up in something you cannot control. You have no power over the choices someone else makes, no matter how many times you tell them how wrong it is. No matter how many times you ask them how could they do this to their own child, this will not change their addiction. An addict's mind registers pain with pleasure, believe me they know what they are doing is WRONG, but their idea of fixing it is by getting high, not by changing their behaviors. Focus on your own relationship with them, learn to use well thought out logic before making assumptions, and focus on ways to help them cope with their past traumas and ways to move forward, instead of worrying about what they are doing involving their drug use.

Another question I hear a lot from people is "what did I do wrong as a parent, and is this my fault?" Well, as I mentioned before, nothing is your fault, unless you physically forced the drug down your child's throat, and I'm hoping that's not the case because if so, this book isn't for you. Like any addiction, more often then none, there are deeper issues indebted within the user that were either not resolved as a child, or continue to take place through adulthood. Addiction is extremely complex, it's usually not the only thing the person is battling. Addiction goes hand in hand with anxiety, depression, bipolar disorder, and other mental illnesses that are often left untreated.

So, when a person is already struggling with one or more of these issues, a drug is just another part of their escape from trying to deal with what they already DON'T know how to deal with (usually being past traumas or other mental illnesses left untreated) therefore, self medicating through drugs becomes the only thing they know how to do. This cycle is referred to something called displacement, and usually everyone's battle with addiction is a result of this. There is another specific behavior that is being ignored or denied and the displacement of drug use becomes the substitute for that missing piece. This just means (something is missing in their life, thus, they replace that feeling with a drug to fill that void.)

Obviously, a person who does not suffer from a mental illness may never understand why trying to find an escape makes sense. But, they don't have to because they aren't fighting something within, that an addict might be fighting. To dig a little deeper into this, a user doesn't just use for the hell of it, they use for many reasons that they might not even realize, justifying using drugs as the answer to their problem. Someone who doesn't suffer from trauma or an underlying illness knows that drugs can deteriorate someone day by day, and KNOWS that drugs are not the answer, because they know that there are other ways to cope with their problems – someone with an addictive personality literally thinks the opposite of this, to them drugs ARE the answer.

To move forward, yes you could have talked to your loved one more about drugs in their youth, yes, you could have been there for your child more, yes, you could have been a more strict parent and had earlier curfews, yes, you could have watched your child's every move, and yes, you could have been a better parent. But, these are all just excuses made by people, after they become addicted to drugs, because believe me, they know this isn't the real reason for their addiction, so don't let them make you think other wise. There are parents who did everything they could, and did everything "right" and their child still became an addict. Do not let them have power over you!

An addict will find a way to get high no matter how close you try and keep them. What we have all discovered is that we cannot stop life from happening. That's a fact. Every single moment, person, and interaction plays apart in someones ability to grow, learn and cope with their experiences. Every single child experiences something different throughout their lives – some a lot worse than others. But, if we always blamed fault and someone else for the reason for everything negative, then there would be a lot more deaths, addicts, crimes, and rapes with adequate excuses for why people do the things they do, with no punishment or consequences.

One of the most important notes to take away from this chapter is to understand that the correlation and link between two factors, does not always necessarily mean that one factor IS the cause of the other. As a society, we have been taught that drugs ARE the reason for why things continue to go wrong, using cause and effect to justify these actions. We blame drugs for poverty, racism, incarceration rates, drug policy, rape, violence and many other negative factors, instead of taking responsibility for finding the root behind these issues individually. Sadly, it's always easier to blame something or someone else for the cause of something negative that is occurring.

To wrap this up, I hope I helped you answer and understand some of the questions you have been searching for. Before you move on, engrave this next little section into your brain in **BOLD** lettering.

No matter how many times your child blames you for their addiction, or blames you for their mistakes, it is still not YOUR fault they decided to pick up the drug and use. When a person blames someone else for their addiction, it is often because they do not know how else to understand their addiction, and because honestly, it's the easier thing to do. Remember, fault and responsibility are two separate things, and every single person has the ability to be responsible for their own life and their own decisions no matter how hard their life is, or was. As a parent or loved one, you have to take responsibility for you own life and your own actions, for that's the ONLY thing you can truly ever control.

Chapter 3: YOU Can't Fix Everything

"Can you please put your phone down and listen to what we have to say ~ for what, all you guys are doing is repeating the same things you have always said to me over and over, I already fucking know"

~ Anonymous

One thing I've noticed over the years is that every single time someone I know talks about their loved one who suffers from addiction with other family or friends, 90 percent of the words that come out of their mouth are negative. Holidays, cherish-able moments and events somehow always revolve around how their son or daughters' drug addiction has ruined their life, and has hurt them so badly. If this sounds like you, THIS HAS TO STOP.

Do you ever stop and wonder why your other kids are more distant from you, why you are so stressed out all the time, or why people don't want to be around you as much as they used too? Well, I'm going to give you a little wake up call. It's because ALL you do is talk about how much you can't do this anymore, how tired and stressed out you are, or you're always talking negatively about your loved ones addiction problem. Your other kids, your friends and your family are tired of everything revolving around this lifestyle. You have got to stop making every holiday or event about them by taking it personal that they don't show up, or come high to it. What's this doing for you by continuing to talk negative about it – besides making yourself more angry, making you crazy, and causing tension between everyone in the room— Nothing, it's doing absolutely nothing for you, besides what I just said. This is why you have to learn to just turn off the crazy emotions for an hour and just be happy they showed up in the first place. Stop asking them if they are high or hammering them about where they have been, or why they are late! Kiss and hug your other kids and tell them how much you love and appreciate them, and do the SAME for your loved one who happens to be an addict, and move on! Your other kids, friends and family need you back in their lives, you have got to stop allowing your loved ones addiction to consume every part of your life, and letting it control your happiness. The next event, party, holiday or birthday you have, try not to bring one negative thing up about this situation, and see how much smoothly and calm the entire day goes. I know it's hard, but you can do this. This one little thing will make your life so much better.

You cannot make them stop, you cannot change them, you cannot control them, you cannot fix everything. If you are like most people, you have asked your loved one over and over again, how could you do this to me? Well, here's something everyone is afraid to tell you, it's not about YOU. No matter how many times you question yourself why your loved one is like this and ask how could this happen to you, the answer will never change. They are not doing this to YOU and will not stop for you. You may be thinking, well after everything you've done for them, how could they steal from you? How could they use in your house? How could they disrespect you? How could they hurt you like this? Well let me help you understand why it is so easy for them to do all of these things when drugs are involved.

First of all, the further an addict dives into this world, the more they lose their connection with their own life. Connections come in all forms, whether it's through love, reality, responsibilities, and even relationships. At each stage of addiction in a users life, connections begin to fade out more and more, and the addict begins to literally lose pieces of who they are, and worse, what they once loved. Because of this, they usually end up isolating themselves from their loved ones, and slowly begin to disassociate one by one from people they once cared for, and instead, turn to people who also use - usually turning to people who they think will understand them, or not judge them.

As healthy relationships begin to dissolve from their lives, new ones begin to take place. Consequently, as I mentioned above, usually replacing old friends with those who also use. Patterns of new "friendships" then begin to form between those of other addicts. These associations with one another are usually based on two things – where to get the drugs, and where to use together. These types of exchanges consist of begging each other to use with one another, pleading and bargaining with one another to get the drug, making each other feel guilty if one uses, and the other isn't, and even feeding off of each others' own high. Getting their fix becomes their reality, their main source of bonding and connecting with one another. They become so attached to the drug, that their main friend, is actually the drug itself, and these new relationships with other addicts are just a part of their path to get high.

Now some of you might be thinking, "well why can't they just stop, if they really wanted too, they could." And, for some, that might hold true. But, one thing I can tell you for sure is that when a drug hits your system, especially opiates, your body begins to crave that high and that high only. Opiates numb all the pain you didn't want to feel, and eventually numb all the pain you do want to feel, too. It takes over you mentally and physically, you lose your ability to really feel anything that you once felt before. The only thing you focus on is the weight of the high to hit your body, and hope that it gets you as high as the time before. The chase becomes something you can see in the distance, but never catch up to. This is called chasing the dragon!!!

The drug makes you feel like it's the only thing you need to be happy and to feel at peace. Those who use for many years often lose the correlation of how to tell the difference between what they want, and what they really need. An addict convinces themselves that all their problems can be solved with a hit. Sadness, depression, sickness, anything that makes them feel like they aren't worthy, they fix with their choice of drug because they are unable to connect reality with actuality. They start to believe that no one loves them or cares for them, they start to truly believe that everyone else around them will never understand their pain, and believe that the drug is the only thing that loves them and does not judge or discriminate against them. Their drug becomes their best friend. Someone they can count on. Someone who will not hurt them. Someone who will not judge them. Someone who can fix them. Their drug of choice helps them to not feel, and to forget any unpleasant experiences in their past. So the thought of stopping, means feeling things you never want to feel again, and is like losing a best friend, and no one wants to lose their best friend.

> " I'm just a piece of shit dope head, I'm never gonna be good as my brother and sister "
>
> ~ Anonymous

Addicts typically project their negative emotions onto others, rather than accepting responsibility. Avoiding reality and denying their problems, lying and stealing, all becomes rationalized in their heads through illogical thinking and justifications, and they will continue this process until they either stop using, or until you change your own behaviors with in this cycle, and stop letting them control you. Thinking you can make them stop by forceful tactics, or believing that you can change them, is only something that will continue to cause arguments and a black whole that will never stop, until YOU stop the cycle. The more you yell, the more you argue, and the more you try to control them, the more they will want to use because it becomes another problem in their life that can easily be resolved by the drug of their choice. Telling them how much they have hurt you, telling them they are ruining their lives, telling them they are going to die, are all things they already know, it's all the things you have said to them repeatedly. Trying to discipline them just pushes them further away, and I know that's not what you want. If you think that being around them more, watching their every move, or you forcing them into listening to you is the answer, you're wrong. Maybe in a perfect world things might change this way, but, sadly, that's not the case in this world.

You cannot expect an addict to want to come around people who are sober because addicts have those very few intimate moments throughout their day to get that feeling they are chasing, and they do not want to be interrupted during this time. If you are the type to continuously try and get your point across to them by yelling at them and putting them down, being around you is the last thing they want because mindset plays a huge part in someones ability to feel the high or not, and if you are ruining that for them, they will stay away as long as they can.

An addict often uses the moments from their previous high during times they are "less high" to try and reminisce on the feeling they felt hours before. They act high, therefore they are high. What a lot of people don't know is that the majority of the feelings an addict has, is a memory, and they use it in other situations so that when they might be coming down, they can still try to continue to feel that chase and high before their next hit.

Addicts also tend to psych themselves out about the feeling of being sick when they cannot get the drug as well. Their mind makes them believe that they NEED the drug or they will get sick without it, even when they are hours away of actually receiving any physical withdrawal symptoms. No user ever wants to experience these symptoms. This to them is worse than death. During this time, anxiety, extreme agitation and false thoughts slowly kick in, making them want and crave the drug even more in hopes to not feel sick. The most challenging part about addiction is that the majority of drug abuse is a huge mental game that they battle with every day, all day. Once they hit a certain point of addiction, it becomes their entire existence, and getting high after a certain point in this lifestyle just becomes a bonus.

Addiction becomes a one person chase, that never ends, and that they can never win, until they stop running. An addict will continue to use until they find their way out of the nightmare. No one else can do this for them. You cannot fix this for them, you cannot fix everything, not this time. Jail doesn't stop an addict, you can't stop an addict, the only thing that stops an addict from using again, IS the addict. You have to learn to stop yelling, stop forcing, and stop creating the same patterns over and over, and instead, understand the reality that you cannot FIX their problem, and that this might be a life long battle for them.

Chapter 4: Nothing Changes, If Nothing Changes

Let me officially start this chapter by saying, OUR justice system was and still is fucked up!!!! Let me tell you a little bit of back history of how disgusting our country was when it came to certain drugs in America. Back in the day, around the late 80's or so, the exploitation of crack cocaine vs. powder cocaine became a wide spread controversy in the south creating a huge increase in black incarceration rates and time served for this offense. The use of drug policy was being used to send a message about race all across the south. Things like violence, crime, damaged families, unemployment, and missing fathers were all being blamed on the use of crack-cocaine, resulting in a disproportionate number of African Americans being sentenced longer for crack cocaine offenses. They literally made longer sentences for those caught with crack cocaine vs. those caught with powder cocaine. Now, obviously crack was cheaper, so it was found in low income communities, and guess who mainly happened to lived there – black families and other communities of color. Unfortunately, because of this misconception of the two drugs, the government convinced people back then to REALLY believe that crack cocaine was the main problem for all of the bad things happening in the world, and if we just got those people off the streets who used this specific drug, and gave them longer prison sentences, things would get better. Well guess what, white rich people were using powder cocaine, and black people were using crack cocaine. Get what I'm saying here? The exploitation of crack cocaine was a strategy to bring white fear into the eye of society, and to further the hatred of black people by making people believe that crack cocaine was worse, so they could hide and justify the secret message behind drug use ~ *let's enslave every black person we can by incarcerating them longer, and in return get free labor out of them, but we will blame it on the crack cocaine use so no one will know the truth.* How disgusting right!?

It was The Anti-Drug Abuse Act of 1986 that implemented the initial disparity, reflecting Congress and the people's view that crack cocaine was a more catastrophic and threatening drug than powder cocaine. Extended research by experts later suggested that the differences between the effects of the two drugs were embellished, and that the sentencing act was completely unjustified. It wasn't until 2010, 20 plus years later, before someone with power actually did something about this. Barack Obama signed The Fair Sentencing Act of 2010, reducing the disparity between the amount of crack cocaine and powder cocaine needed to trigger certain federal criminal penalties, and eliminated the five-year mandatory minimum sentence for simple possession of crack cocaine.

https://www.ncbi.nlm.nih.gov/pmc/articles/PMC4533860/#!po=15.1316

Anyway, as you've noticed, not too much has changed. The justice system still is pretty fucked up today. Let me explain why from my own experience. I come from a small community, and not one time have I ever heard of a place, organization or resource that helps those who struggle with addiction. Instead, they put these people in jail for 20-30 days (where they are still able to use because people sneak in needles that they pass around) and then they come out and do the exact same thing they did before. There is no system set up in place for these people to succeed after incarceration. It just becomes a vicious cycle. They go on probation, break it, and go back to jail. They come out, use, break their probation once again, and go right back to jail, often leading to overdoses because users go back to the same amount of drugs they were putting into their bodies as before. My brother and cousin have gone through this exact process probably 30 times combined, and not one time did anyone offer them real help or even give them resources to get help. And, not one time has this "solution" stopped either of them from going and using again.

Heroin addiction among young adults between the ages 18-25 has doubled in the past ten years. About 14.5 million adults 26 and older struggle with a substance abuse disorder. Almost twice as many people who are unemployed struggle with addiction than those who work full time. About half of the population in the American prisons and jail systems suffer from addiction, while 75 percent of those who struggle, also suffer from mental illnesses. I could go on an on with statistics, but that's not going to change anything, especially for a struggling community who is losing their loved ones to addiction.

That is a lot of fucking people with a drug problem!! So where is the money for this solution really going? Who is this money actually helping? What is the justice system doing to help this epidemic? These are the big questions a lot of people wonder about whose child suffers from drug addiction, but has never been offered any real help. Believe me, I wish I knew that answer myself, but I don't. What I do know, is that in most small communities, their solution to the drug problem is letting the little fish go (small time drug dealers and addicts) because jails are too full, and in return, has hope that one of the small time felons will snitch and lead them to the king drug dealer. Now don't get me wrong, I see the point in why this would be a smart tactic for the police, but when something isn't working in your community, don't you think it's time to take a different route? For example, maybe taking into consideration about all of the people dying every other week from overdoses, or families being torn apart by drug addiction in the process. Shouldn't our justice system be redirecting their thoughts and actions into answers that actually bring real solutions? Maybe start with asking themselves "is that king drug dealer really worth losing another young adult over?"

Absolutely not, it's not worth it! And you might be thinking it's not that simple, the police are just doing their job. Well, they aren't doing their "job" very well because I've seen this actually happen. I've seen police let addicts and small time drug dealers back on the streets with no hesitation, and without offering any kind of help because all they care about is the big time dealer. Well guess what, an addict will just find another way to get the drugs if their main source (the big fish) is locked up, and someone else will just step up to the plate and become the head dealer, if the opportunity is given to them. The war on drugs is never going to change. Sadly, this is how our justice system functions, and it's killing our children, friends and families.

The war on drugs has taken place since the early 1960's and for the past nearly 60 years, it has failed to produce any real form of success in slowing down incarnation and death rates. One person in the Portland Metro area dies every other day from a drug overdose. The way we see drugs must change, and it starts with the way we understand this problem, and how to cope with it ourselves. By focussing more attention on the positive solutions (such as creating community centers or opening more treatment facilities) the community, court systems and local police can work better together by providing faster, more effective improvements for the lives of youth and young adults who suffer with addiction, and, also help the prevention of it. Creating better plans, more places to go for addicts to feel safe, a better organized community, and more funding towards this epidemic is the only thing that will help slow it down. The community at hand, has to better prepare themselves in order to create real change. As a loved one of a user, you have to learn to see other ways around it. You cannot change the rules, but what you can do is focus only on what you can control, and that's your own relationship with you and your loved ones addiction.

So, with that being said, the only advice I can give to you in this mess is to change your own view on it, or nothing will change. For example, If getting more involved is something you do want to do, you can start by encouraging your local news media to actually talk about the crisis that is happening, and empower those who want to make a difference in the outcomes of this epidemic to come together to help create real change. On top of that, do your research on the drug statistics in your own city or state, so that you can be better equipped to talk about it openly with others who also might be struggling with this fight. This is a huge stepping stone in creating change with in your own fight because others around you might know of resources you didn't know about before hand. Don't be afraid to talk about your loved ones addiction, stop letting it consume your life, realize that the justice system probably won't change, and start taking matters into your own hands by being involved with your loved ones addiction as much or as little as YOU want to be.

For so many, the shame and embarrassment of being the parent or friend of someone who uses stops them from reaching out for help. The stigma around this lifestyle must change, and learning to talk openly with others about where you can go for resources or where you can get the help you might be looking for, might just be the answer you need, and might just help play apart in saving your child's life.

You cannot stop the addict from using by yourself. When better solutions with in this lifestyle exist, it will provide the user with more opportunity and more of a reason to stay clean in the long run, if they do ever decide to stop. If you are someone who wants to help make a real difference, you have to take real steps in getting there. Don't be afraid to reach out!!

Chapter 5: A Year In Their Shoes

At this point, I can only guess that those who are reading my book are wondering why and how I know so much about addiction, and why I am able to openly talk about it with others. Let me start by saying that this isn't exactly what I ever thought I would be doing with my life. But, when an opportunity came up to help change the lives of others, I immediately wanted to dive in, and this was the best way I knew how too. In life sometimes your calling finds you, instead of you finding it, and I knew that by using my platform and not being afraid to tell the truth about addiction, it would allow me to help so many other people who continue to be in a position I was once in myself. I hope my story and experience proves to you that you are not alone, and helps you find the answers you are searching for.

I have lost people who are still alive. I had to do something different. I knew that if nothing changed about the cycle my mind went through while trying to process the reasoning behind my loved ones addiction, that I would eventually end up driving myself crazy. I could no longer endure upon sleepless nights. I could no longer cry myself to sleep. I could no longer question myself, blame myself or go through the emotional and physical pain that my loved ones put me through. But, most of all, I could no longer watch my family suffer by always thinking and believing that "this time will be different." If NOTHING changes, than NOTHING changes, so, I finally took it upon myself to understand addiction the best way I knew how, and that was by trying to feel what they felt.

Before I get into all the details about what I did to get where I am today, let me start by telling you WHY I did what I did. As a young teenager, I started noticing more and more that my life was a lot different than my friends lives. My mom was a single mom with 3 kids, I grew up in the "ghetto" on food stamps and house vouchers, and someone in my family was always getting into some kind of trouble. As time went on, it became normal to move from house to house; well apartment to apartment and school to school usually because my brothers' addiction did not allow us to move to certain places and we were always getting kicked out of houses because of his drug use. So nothing really ever felt stable. It became normal for my life to be chaotic, if something wasn't going wrong, it felt quiet and weird. I needed disruption to feel at ease. My cousins were heroin addicts, my dad, his mom and dad, my great aunt and uncle were all drug addicts. It was just apart of my life. This was my reality, and I didn't know how to separate the two.

On the weekends, I would spend my days usually in Portland, Oregon at my grandmas' house or my great aunts' house because I wasn't really allowed to be around my dad, well actually more like he just didn't want anything to do with my brother and I. As a young child, my form of "play" was going to the cemetery late at night to steal flowers off of people's graves to make money. Stuff like that was normal to me because I didn't know other kids didn't do that. During the times I would stay there, I would see so many people coming in and out and always was so curious to why they had so "many friends" coming in and out all hours of the day, I was so naive.

At a young age, I realized that even though my dad was alive, I had lost him to drugs long before I could understand the affects that came from the drugs he was putting into his body. As I got a little older though, I started to understand addiction in a new way, and I knew I could never hold my dad accountable for not being a good father, when he fathered my brother and I during his addiction. We were never in his plan and we were never supposed to happen, we came from something that would only get in the way of his daily routine, which like most addicts, consisted of getting high, or finding a way to get high. Me and my brother didn't fit in that sequence, and his own dad was a drug addict and in and out of prison for identity theft, so again his upbringing was a lot different than most - not giving my dad an excuse to be a piece of shit, but it makes more sense now.

Anyway, when my brother and I were younger, we didn't REALLY understand that he was an addict, or why he didn't want us in his life. How could we? My brother and I were just kids, fatherless, and the only thing we knew and could feel was that our dad didn't want anything to do with us. Let me just tell you it's a feeling I couldn't shake for a really long time, no matter how many times I tried, or how hard I tried to understand why my own father didn't love me, it stayed with me for years until recently. It took me putting myself through hell not only for myself, but for my brother as well, just to try and understand why using was more important than us.

From the age of 16 on, it seemed like everyone close to me was turning to drugs. My brother, my dad, my cousins, my friends, my boyfriend. Everyone I loved, cared for, or needed, their lives revolved around drugs. I hated it. I hated what it was doing to them, I hated how it made them act, but even worse, I hated what it was doing to me. I felt like I was losing control. Year after year would go by, but nothing ever changed. I continued to see my loved ones destroy their bodies and their minds every single day. I watched heroin take my family by the throat and suck the life out of them. It didn't matter how many times I tried to talk to them about their addiction, it never stopped. Mentally, my loved ones were losing their grasps with reality. Nothing was more important to them besides getting high. I watched them all turn in to monsters, and turn into the exact person they never wanted to be like. My brother became my dad. He became someone who only cared about himself, who blamed others for all of his actions, and who abandoned his daughter and son, just like my dad did with us. Every single time I would have a deep conversation with my brother, he always told me that the main reason why he uses is because of our dad. He too was so lost and confused on why the man who made us, didn't want us, but then turned around and was doing the same exact thing to his own kids. Now that was something that made me want to understand addiction even more. My dad was the first one to give my brother heroin, and that was the only bonding experience they ever shared together. The cycle of addiction around me continued for years, it was the only thing I knew, and I needed answers and a different solution.

Everyday I was living in fear that I would physically lose someone I loved. If I wasn't worried about my brother, I was worried about my cousins, if I wasn't worried about my cousins I was worried about my boyfriend, if I wasn't worried about my boyfriend I was worried about my friends. My entire life was surrounded by addiction. I watched the man I loved go from being the smartest person I ever knew, to someone I could no longer recognize. My close guy friends, my boyfriend at the time, and my brother all started hanging out, and being young and naive, I thought this was awesome. What could be better? Everyone you love getting along and spending time together, it was something I always wanted. But, when I was no longer being invited places and was hearing stories about what they were doing and who they were hanging out with, I started to realize that their bonding was formed solely based on the desire to get high off of heroin with each other. And, because I loved all of them and they knew how hurt I would be if I found out, they hid their addiction from me and refused to tell me what kind of stuff they were all doing together. The one person who hid it from me the most was my significant other at the time, he would go above and beyond to make any excuse for why he was acting the way he was, and why he was always gone. For awhile, I believed him because I loved him, and I never in my wildest dreams thought HE would turn to heroin, especially after seeing what it had done to my family members. But, being around it so much before him, it didn't take me long to read the signs that he too was addicted, and that's when everything in my life went south. I seriously started feeling like I was going crazy. Having one addict around you is tough, trying having 6, all telling me different things, lying so well that I think they all convinced themselves that their lies were actually true. I never knew what was real and what wasn't. I was being warped into their world because I didn't know how to separate myself from them, all I wanted to do was help them, and change them, but the addiction was too strong.

I would hear that one of my friends and my boyfriend were pimping girls, I would hear that someone I loved overdosed and came back to life by his friends hitting him over and over, I would find needles in backpacks, I would hear from people that my loved ones were sleeping with girls for money, that they were selling and cutting drugs up to make a profit to buy more drugs. Believe me, this is just the basic stuff that I saw and knew they were doing. Addicts live an unspoken world that is almost unbelievable if you knew who they were before the drugs. They would literally almost do anything just to get high, no matter how much it was against their morals or how disgusting it was, at the time it was their survival kits, and they all knew how to manipulate, lie and use people until they got exactly what they wanted. It was a game to them. And in their heads, for awhile they were winning. They had money, they had girls, they had drugs, they had each other. But, like most people who use, they never thought it would completely take control of who they were and slowly drown them one by one. They all thought they were invincible, not knowing prison and jail were right around the corner, and that's exactly what happened to most of them.

I couldn't watch or it be around it anymore. After a few years of nonstop battling to try and get them to stop, I convinced my boyfriend at the time to move away from the city that was tearing everyone apart. You have no idea how happy I was when he said yes, in my head I truly believed this was going to be a new start for us. Taking him away from the people who fed his addiction, and taking him somewhere where no one knew him so we could both start fresh, never imagining what would happen next. The next few months became the saddest, most difficult times of my life. I watched the man who I thought I was going to marry, the man who I was most connected to in this world, mentally and physically die in front of my eyes. His addiction became his entire life, and I wasn't enough to stop him. Love wasn't enough, and in most cases, it never will be. The fights and arguments got so bad that I would kick him out and feel like I was having heart attacks from the stress I was going through. Doctors even ended up putting me on Xanax because he was never home, and I was having other drug addicts come to the door at three, four in the morning asking for him, making me question my every move. I felt so scared for my own life everyday. The neighbors were always so high on meth that I could hear them at all hours doing the most random shit, and they were constantly telling me how bad my ex was getting into meth now, and how much he lies to me about it. I would find needles all over my apartment and in my laundry. I started drowning with him because I thought I could change him, everyday the situation became more hostile. My life was quickly coming unraveled.

I became obsessed with trying to fix him, and all it was doing was hurting both of us. I was doing things that were completely out of character. I would scream at the top of my lungs and go over to the neighbors house with a bat and threaten them with it if they didn't shut the fuck up, or tell me where he was. There was one time I got so mad that I threw a glass cup at the wall and stood on our glass coffee table and stomped on it and shattered it into pieces. I was addicted to chaos, I thought the crazier I acted, the more it would scare him into stopping. The cops would come to our apartment and I would have scratches all over my body from wrestling around with my significant other. I would have to lie to them about what was going on every time. My entire life had been based around one chaotic cycle of addiction, mental and physical abuse, that when anything normal or right would happen, I couldn't handle it or believe it. All I was doing was making myself go insane. This stage in my life didn't last long though, I could only take so much of actually being in the lifestyle and seeing it at hand, instead of just being an outsider and hearing about it.

After about 3 months of complete turmoil, there was a time when he didn't come home for 3 days and I couldn't take the pain and uncertainty if he was alive or not anymore. I rode my bike in 18 degree weather for 3 hours looking for him, and when I found him, I never imagined what would happen next. I saw his truck parked outside of a hotel, the thoughts going through my head at the time were ludicrous, I impatiently started knocking on all of the doors of the hotel like I was a fucking maid until finally I found him. He wouldn't come out, and the girls inside there with him kept telling me to leave. Finally, after telling him I wasn't going anywhere, he came out after about 20 minutes. I was fucking freezing, shaking, and so full of hate. I will never forget the shame and look in his eyes, as if he didn't know that I knew what had been going on for years. He could barely look at me, I could finally see and feel the guilt and humiliation on his face. He just kept looking at me.

We got into his car, and he just started driving. He told me he would never be able to forgive himself for what I just had to witness, this was the first time we had talked in days. I don't think I had ever cried so much in my life. He drove me back to the house and came inside and sat with me for an hour. I thought that maybe me seeing him like this would finally make him stop. I begged him not to leave the house again because I felt like someone was after me, and all he could do was say "I'm sorry sadie," and he kissed me, and left back out the door. I was sick.

I couldn't even believe it. He was so far gone, that he was willing to lose me over a substance. I was so heartbroken. I knew it was finally time. It was time to let go. I frantically started packing up my stuff after he left, and when I went to look under the bed to see if I had left anything, I saw a wedding ring box. I just sat there shook. Mentally, I was so disoriented that I just sat there for like 30 minutes and stared at it. I never ended up opening it. I was so numb.

I left the next day without ever saying bye to him or letting him know I was leaving, after being with him for five years. Talk about pain and constant regret. It was the hardest decision I have ever had to make in my entire life, but I knew I could no longer live this lifestyle. I had so much love for this man, I told myself I would never give up on him no matter what he ever did to me. But, I gave up. Love wasn't enough to keep me tangled in his web of destruction. I couldn't take it anymore. I left the very next day not knowing if I would ever see the only person I ever loved, ever again. This is when I finally knew that NO one can stop addiction, except the addict themselves.

A couples years had went by and during this time my life just seemed to exist. All I ever worried about was if my ex was okay or not, and I questioned my decision to leave him everyday. All I could think about was how could I leave this man when he needed me the most. I became so distant from everyone and everything because I felt like I had lost the most important person in my life. On top of that, My brother was still using, my cousins were in prison, I still struggled with identity issues brought on by my friends and family, and I was more devastated than ever about how my life was turning out. The pain from the memories of him, and the strenuous wondering if my brother would ever stop using, still seemed to take over my existence. As if that wasn't already enough, during this time, my grandpa who was my best friend and the only person I really considered my dad, had passed in July of 2016. This ripped a hole through me. I didn't know how much more I could take. Losing my grandpa made everything worse, not only for me but for my entire family. Everyone lost a piece of them that day, and my family started getting worse and worse. I began to feel more detached from life than ever. I had lost the only two men who ever loved me. I was so lost.

A couple months after my grandpa's passing, the unthinkable happened. I got the text. "He's dead." He overdosed. I'll never forget the flood of emotions that immediately came over my body. My friend, and ex boyfriends' brother overdosed on the one drug tearing everyone I loved apart. He was gone forever. I would never see him or hear his laugh ever again. All I can remember doing was going into the bathroom and dropping to my knees in the shower and crying so hard that I didn't know if I was ever going to be able to stop. I was so sad, but mostly scared for what my ex would do next. All I wanted to do was help him and be there for him more after this, but he didn't want to talk to anyone after he lost his brother. My stomach was in knots for weeks. When I saw my ex at the funeral, I barely recognized him. Not even losing a brother could stop his drug abuse.

A few weeks had went by and realization started to hit me harder than ever. And, If you are thinking that the same won't eventually happen to you, you're wrong. It's only a matter of time before addiction affects everyone around you, including you, whether you are an addict or a loved one. Addiction was ripping my life apart from the inside out, and I wasn't even the one using. I couldn't take it anymore. I had to do something different. I had to try and understand it.

Three months after my friends funeral, I started really reevaluating my life and searching for answers. This finally gave me the solution I was looking for. I knew what I needed to do with my life. It's crazy to think that it took death to get me there, but it did. I packed my entire apartment up and drove my car and u-haul down to Las Vegas.

Now, what I am about to tell you next, you may believe and you may not, but it's the truth. I attempted something that I would never hope any one else would ever try themselves to find answers. I isolated myself from everyone I knew, my plan was to try and understand addiction the only way I knew how, and I knew Las vegas was the place to do it. *I tried to understand the mind of an addict the only way I knew how, and that was to try to become a "temporary" one.*

A lot of you might be thinking I'm crazy at this point. You're probably asking questions like why would someone ever do something like this knowing the risks? Well for one, I was desperate for my life to change. And for two, I was heavily inspired by the 2004 documentary *Supersize Me* where Morgan Spurlock did a 30 day trial on the effects of what fast food (McDonald's) does to someones' body. I wanted to do something similar, so I took it upon myself to take pain pills everyday for a year to see how it would effect me mentally and physically. Sounds demented right? Well, I was at a point in my life where I didn't and couldn't see any other options, and, if it worked out for me, I knew that my findings and own experience might be able to help someone else down the road understand addiction better, too. I had no idea what I was getting myself into, but I was ready and wasn't going to turn back now. I knew I was taking a risk by doing what I was doing, but I had to find the answers I was searching for.

Anyway, before I go into my own experience with how pain pills affected me, as you can see, for so many years, I had allowed other people's lifestyle choices to completely ruin my own life. There was no one telling me to stop yelling at them. There was no one telling me to stop trying to change them. In my head, I truly believed that I could stop them from using if I just tried harder. Everyone around me was allowing my family's drug use to take over our lives and drain us dry, until we had nothing left. We didn't know how to make it stop until finally I made a change with in myself. I do not want you ending up like my family, or doing what I did! You have to make a change TODAY towards this destructive web of addiction, or 10 years from now you will be dealing with the same problems you face today.

Chapter 6: Taking A Risk

It's easy as an outsider, and a non-user to blame someone else for their loved ones addiction. No matter how many times you see them high, or how many times they steal from you, somehow you still convince yourself that if they just didn't hang out with that certain person, if they lived in a different city, if their drug dealer got caught, or if their mom or dad hadn't been a drug addict themselves, that they wouldn't be this way. Well, it doesn't work that way. An addict will find a way to get high no matter who they are around, no one else controls their desire to get high, but them. Don't get me wrong, someone else's addiction that your loved one might hang around definitely helps feed their addiction more, and the lifestyle someone lived before their drug use plays a huge factor in the predisposition phase as well, but other people, and outside factors do not determine their fate. The only person who can control addiction, is the person themselves. The more you believe and convince yourself that it is someone else's fault for your loved ones drug problem, the less likely you will take responsibility for your own actions and thoughts towards them, and you will continue to let the person you love not fully take responsibility for their drug use as well, just reassuring them that it's okay to make excuses for it, just like you are for them.

Everyone puts themselves at risk for anything they do, whether it's addiction, over eating, excessive exercising, we as human beings must take our own responsibility and actions into our own hands, we are the only ones to blame for our decisions. Now, with that being said, we must remember that addiction affects everyone differently, and we cannot expect one person to be like someone else. Addiction all comes down to the user themselves. Nothing is more powerful than your own mind, UNLESS you allow it to be.

At any age, it can be hard to identify the point where drugs cross over from recreational, to addiction. The fact is, at any moment, whether someone uses once in awhile, or everyday, they put themselves at risk for developing a dependency, even if they don't see it or feel it themselves at first. It often takes someone months or even years to realize that they even have a problem. Everybody experiences a drug a little bit different than someone else, one person might be able to take a drug and never take it ever again. Others, may take it once, and be hooked for life. That's the reality of addiction, there is no exact cause for why it effects people more than others.

As an outsider of addiction, your main concern should only be WHY your loved one picked up the drug in the first place, to then try and set up success for recovery in the long run, instead of trying to FIX the actual drug problem itself in that moment. Education, pressuring them, and forceful tactics alone are not enough to help the addict get clean, and everyday they use they are putting themselves at a higher risk for further dependency. The main thing to focus on as an outsider of addiction is how to cope with it yourself by taking a step back, understanding that you alone cannot fix or change them, and by taking the blame off of yourself. You have to come to terms with the reality that an addict will use no matter what until they are ready to stop, and realize that what you say or do to try and convince them otherwise is just going to put more strain on your own life. You do not HAVE to let addiction control your life too, only if you let it.

Anyway, for me, I knew that with my families history of drug abuse, I couldn't tell anyone what I was doing in regards to my experiment because I didn't want to worry them. My entire life before this, I had stayed away from drugs and alcohol because I knew with my genetic back ground and predisposed environment surrounding addiction, that I could potentially be at a higher risk for the feeling and urge to use. On top of that, I knew it would always be super easy to get drugs if I did want them, especially since I had been around it my entire life, and it was all that I really knew. I understood that I needed to be extremely careful and thoughtful about the relationship I would soon have with these pain pills. Knowing how addiction affects all walks of life- rich, poor, children of addicts, men and women, I knew that addiction did not discriminate. For me, it was a little bit different trying to actually plunge into this lifestyle because I knew that other factors would play a part in my ability to try and understand addiction. Because my mind had always been so strong, I wasn't sure that I would be able to feel what others had felt during their drug use. Another thing that made it a little bit harder for me to understand the different drug phases, was the fact that I actually needed the pain pills. My body was like a 900 day old cookie ready to crumble at any moment with all my body issues. Trying to distinguish the difference of when I needed to take the pain pills due to real pain, or when I had the feeling of just wanting to take them for fun, made it really difficult for me to know if it was my mind playing tricks on me, or not. I found that this became a huge dilemma through out my journey. One thing I did notice right away was that I started to feel the pills take away my feelings a little more as the days went on. I will go a little more into that in the next few chapters.

If you have read anything about addiction online, you have probably came across the stages of drug dependency. Those consist of tolerance, psychological dependence, physical dependence and of course, addiction. Tolerance is when your body gets used to a certain amount of the drug you are taking, and you feel yourself needing more of it to achieve the same amount of high as before. Psychological dependence is when you have gotten so used to the sensation the drug brings you, that your mind starts to remember and crave that pleasure, often resulting in feeling on edge if you cannot take the drug. Physical dependence is when the withdrawal symptoms kick in. You experience unpleasant reactions such as sweating, vomiting, shaking and nausea when you stop using the drug. Last, comes addiction. This is different for everybody. Addiction is a widespread controversy, usually resulting in the compulsive need to seek and obtain drugs. This phase often leads to a more dangerous lifestyle, along with the disintegrating havoc it brings to the users mind, body and relationships. In my next couple chapters, I will be explaining my own experience of these stages in more detail so that someone who has never seen or physically felt any of these phases themselves can have a better understanding of the process of drug use.

Chapter 7: I Was A Zombie Without It

During my year long experiment, I was slowly starting to understand the power of drugs a little more everyday. I started to question my decision to continue with my study more and more. I would walk around so slow and sluggish everywhere I went, I felt like a zombie. I still can sit here and remember the feeling of extreme exhaustion that would come over my body if I didn't have a pill in my system. I would walk into work and lay my head on the table and feel so dull, lifeless, and completely expressionless. It was like nothing creative or passionate would ever come to my brain. I could see and hear everyone, but it was like I was underwater drowning out the all noises. One way I like to describe this to people is by telling them to cover both of their ears tightly for an entire minute and to have someone talk to them. Try it now!

Weird sensation right? That's how I was starting to feel everyday! People would try talking to me and I would find myself asking them "huh" like 2 or 3 times during a conversation because I couldn't focus on anything. I would start to feel anxious and unbalanced if didn't take any pills, and even would try so hard not to take them while I worked, but every single time, and I mean every single time, I would somehow convince myself to go take some, or convince myself that my body needed them for pain. 30 minutes after taking them would go by and it was literally like a light switch in my body would flick on, and my head would pop up above water. I could see and hear clearly again.

My mind went from Portland Oregon Weather In December to Los Angeles weather in the summer. Everything became clear, bright and loud again, it was bizarre. I have no idea how no one ever noticed at work because my personality would go from angry Robert De Niro to Kevin Hart in a matter of minutes. I would start talking, and be all over the place, the messed up part was is that I aways made more money when I would take them because it gave me way more energy to do my job better. So for me, this is what made it so challenging for me to establish the difference between if I just really thoroughly enjoyed the pleasure pain pills were giving me, or if I was in so much pain that they were giving me my quality of life back. It started really fucking with my head because I knew that most people who use opiates get the opposite feeling of what I was experiencing when I was on them (nodding off, feeling tired, in slow motion, etc) compared to the liveliness they brought me. At the same time though, I could still feel them starting to partially take control of my mind and body, even if my results from them were different than someone else's. This is when I knew that the psychological phase of dependence was becoming a huge factor in my research, and made me pay closer attention to how my body was reacting to the pills. I was starting to physically become so used to the excitement the drug was bringing me, that my mind began craving this sensation more through out the day. When I didn't take any, my body was left feeling like the walking dead, awake, but extremely comatosed.

It's like my mind was slowly rewiring itself. The only thing that began to give me motivation to do anything, was the thought of the pills. My body would ache without them, but my mind was yearning for them for pleasure, so trying to distinguish the difference between what was real, and what my mind was fabricating, became a huge controversy between me and my own thoughts.

It was like the pills gave me powers. They made me want to go and be more social, they helped me workout, they consistently aided me into doing my job more sufficiently, and they gave me way more energy. They made me the person I thought I wanted to be on the inside.

Ah, but on the other hand, for quite some time I couldn't see that they were sucking my personality away from me one day at a time. I didn't really notice how bad they were affecting my personality until one day I hadn't taken any pills yet, and one of my co-workers/friend said to my boss " at least I have a personality, unlike sadie." This is when it really hit me that I was really starting to lose a piece of who I was before this. She was right. When I wasn't on the pills, I never had anything to say and would just sit there quiet and dumbfounded. I swear it's like they were taking my intelligence away.

This became another tremendous battle I faced because I needed them for my back and aching body, but without them I was starting to feel miserable mentally and physically. In my head, I knew that they were allowing me to live the life of a 26 year, so the process of my experiment felt so lopsided at times because every part of me wanted to believe that my body and mind wasn't actually feeling the negative effects of the pills, and instead, they were just giving me the quality of life I deserved. To this day, I will always wonder if it was my mind playing tricks on me and wonder if I really needed them for the pain I was feeling, or if my body was just beginning to crave it's form of power back that the pills were giving me.

After a few months of taking pills everyday, it became a normal day to day habit for me. It was like eating, or getting dressed, it became a routine to me that fit into my everyday schedule. When you do something for so long, your body becomes accustomed to it, your choices turn into habits, and your habits turn into routines. I would wake up, shower, get dressed, eat, take pills, go to work. Repeat. It was just a normal part of my day after awhile, even if I didn't even want to take them, or if I barely felt any satisfaction from them. A time of the day would hit, usually about 4pm, and my mind would literally remind me to take them; they were just apart of me at this point.

For someone who has never experienced the feeling your body feels when it wants a drug after a long day, let me try and explain. The best way I can describe the "warmness" that it would bring me is to try to imagine being really sore all over your body and not having a cold, but feeling like you're going to get one very soon. Then combine that with a time you only had one hour of sleep before one of your work shifts, and you worked 20 hours the day before. Now, Imagine how your body feels after that long day of all of this stuff fused together - sluggish, tired, slow, sick feeling, irritated, on edge.

Now, imagine that same night after that long day, you go to a professional massage parlor. You lay on the soft table in preparation for smooth soft hands to hit your body. Okay, now picture someone's hands rubbing your tired body in a nice, quiet, dim lighted room, and that rapid sigh of relief you get as they start massaging your sore and lethargic body. It feels amazing right? That's how it feels the minute a drug kicks in after a long day without it. Your body lets out a sigh of relief, as the tension and miserable feeling you felt, starts to slowly dissolve.

Well, an addicts' mind and body goes through this phase everyday if they can't get their drug of choice, and the only way they know how to fix the pain and sickness they are feeling, is by getting that sigh of relief through pleasure - through drugs, just to feel normal again.

Surprisingly during my experience, I never felt REAL withdrawal systems - night sweats, nausea, aching, body aches vomiting etc. For me, since I wasn't taking that many pills a day and wouldn't allow myself to take more, thankfully, I only mentally reached the psychological stage, which made me believe that I needed them for energy and thinking that they would make me feel better, rather than reaching the actual "addiction" phase.

Through out my experiment, I never reached the final stage (addiction). But, like with anything, drugs affect people differently, I would not allow myself to reach the addiction phase no matter how bad I wanted more pain pills during that time, my mind would not let me take more. Don't get me wrong though, I didn't reach that phase because I wanted to be done with the experiment, not because I didn't want more or crave more. Because to be quite honest, I did want more at times. But, I was DONE on my own time, I knew it was time to stop, so I did. No one was going to change my mind, and I wouldn't of listened to anyone if they had told me to stop. So believe me, now I can see and feel WHY other people form addictions and can't stop, because that shit can be the devil if your mind is weak. It calls you. It reminds you of the feeling, and it feels so good, until it slowly takes pieces of you day by day if you let it. I just chose not to let it. I am the exception in most cases.

Before I go into the next chapter, I want my readers to understand one thing about continued drug use first. Just because someone uses a drug regularly, does not automatically make them an addict, and it doesn't even mean that person has a drug problem. According to the *American psychiatric association*, addiction is a complex condition - a brain disease that is manifested by compulsive substance use despite harmful consequence. People with addiction (severe substance use disorder) have an intense focus on using a certain substance(s), such as alcohol or drugs, to the point that it takes over their life. They keep using alcohol or a drug even when they know it will cause problems.

For me, because of the disease I was born with, pills are the only thing that makes my body feel somewhat normal. Yes they have the ability to "change" how I am feeling, but I will never be an addict because it does not affect my life negatively, I do not seek out drugs, I do not take them everyday, and I possess too much self love to ever go down that road. I have never had the desire to want or need more, as a reader you must know the difference.

https://www.psychiatry.org/patients-families/addiction/what-is-addiction

Chapter 8: It Took My Pain Away, I Think

You're probably wondering by now how I was able to get so many pain pills in my possession to do something like this. Well let me explain. About 6 years ago, around the age of 20, I was diagnosed with Pars defect, and Ehlers Danlos-syndrome (hypermobility). From the age of 14 on, all I really knew was pain. But, when you are poor, and live in a small town, you don't really have many options when it comes to good doctors. I was an athlete, and not just one who played for fun, I played all year long. Sports were my life, and everything I did revolved around them. Because of my conditions, and not knowing I had them at the time, I battled with multiple injuries throughout my sports career, eventually resulting in a career ending injury effecting my spine. For years I knew something wasn't right with my body. I was always hurting, always in the training room, always given pain pills. Sports were everything to me though - my way into college, my escape, and my entire identity. So, when my coaches asked if I was okay to play, my answer was always yes, knowing I wasn't. How do you say no when you're told by your coaches, peers and even teammates that you would be letting your team down if you don't play, or that you would lose your scholarship if you sit out, or even that you are useless to the team if you're injured? You do this by convincing yourself that you're fine, and that the pain will go away if you help your team win, and so you take another pain pill, and lace your shoes up for your game.

After a few years of constant battling with injuries and severe pain, I finally went to the doctor to see what was really wrong with me. When I was told I could no longer play the sports that I loved, it felt like I had been punched in the stomach by Dwayne the Rock Johnson. I was sick about it. I just sat in the doctors office and my mind went into outer space. All I could think about is what the F am I going to do now. I was so confused. I felt like my life was ending. I felt like I was being trapped inside a 90 year old's body. I always just thought that everyone experienced pain from sports, and everyone else was hurting too. I never imagined that all my pain was because of the conditions I was born with.

Next thing I knew the doctor started prescribing me all these pills. I was getting nerve pain medicine, muscle relaxers, butrans patches, and of course, pain medicine. I had been prescribed pain medicine before, so I knew a little bit about them obviously because some of my previous injuries, but, they were always in small amounts and refills didn't exist - all this other shit was super new to me. I left the doctors office that day wondering if my quality of life would ever be the same.

When I first was prescribed the pain medicine, I was taking them about every 4 days to a week. And usually only after workouts or to help me sleep. Sometimes I would even go months without taking them.

When I first started taking them consistently during my time spent in Vegas, (during my 1 year experiment) the first 3 to 4 months felt pretty normal, and they were just being used for my pain. I could take 1-2 and get a small buzz from them and it would make my pain pretty low, so they were doing what was expected from them. But, after about month 5, I starting to feel them take a toll on me, in ways that scared me more than I had ever been scared in my life. I remember laying in bed and thinking to myself, am I even in pain anymore, or do I just want more pills. There were times that I felt extreme pain, but knew I only had enough pills to last a certain amount of days, so I had to choose between pain, or feeling a better buzz. I knew they were starting to effect my control and tolerance for them when I would wait to be in less pain, so that the pills would work better on me. This was my beginning stage of building tolerance. My body was getting used to the certain amount of pills

I was consuming, so everyday I wanted to take a little bit more because not only were 1 or 2 not giving me a buzz anymore, now they weren't taking my pain away either. This is how I knew tolerance was a real thing.

I tried so hard to feel something from 1 or 2 pills, that I would even eat less to feel the effects more, and I would even wait a full 24 hours to take the pills the next day to see if I would get better results from them. But, that amount was just not giving me the outcome it had before. At least it seemed that way in my head. The tolerance stage was the start to my body and mind literally changing how I felt, and what I felt. There were times that I would lay in my bed with all the lights off and write poem after poem to try and get out what my body was feeling. The only way I really knew how to do that was to write shit down, I always called it my "notes full of substance." It was the only way I felt intelligent again. I could feel them starting to take my passions, dedication and excitement away from me, or maybe they were giving that part of my life back to me when I was on them that had been taken from me due to chronic pain.

There's one poem that I wrote when I was on them, that when I read it today it makes me sick to even think that my mind was thinking this way. It went like this;

Pain or pleasure by Sadie Petersen
It's not that I think about it, I'm lying because I do. It's my go to.
Who can I reach out to without scaring them? I don't know what
to do. I don't know why I chose you. when I'm feeling anxious, in
pain, sad, nervous, I reach in my bag knowing it's always gonna be
there. It's helped
me through almost every uncomfortable situation,
every time I feel fear, have sex, work, even interviews, I don't re-
member the real me when I'm around someone new.
I think I've convinced myself it's not real because I need it, taking
them every single day, always counting and making sure I have
enough to get me through the days.

Pain still wins sometimes, And it might always. But, now it's not just back pain, these seem to have mentally taken its toll now too.

My personality changes, they give me energy. That's not normal behavior, so I'm fine right?

I barely feel a high anymore, is this the real me they are bringing out of me, just without all the pain and suffering? It's hard to tell the difference.

Before my body started failing me, I do remember being happy, without these.

But now, I'm like a walking zombie before I reach in my bag pull out pills and wait for the light, I for sure know this can't be right. So what do I do?

How do I separate the two? I don't feen for them now, what's gonna happen if I ever do?

I don't start to feel sick without them, but I do know they are apart of me now.

I know the effects they give other people helps them become numb, but I really think for me it's different.

So I ask myself do I have a problem? I feel so dumb.

I take them away and my body aches. I cry because I'm scared. With or without them I feel fear.

Am I helping my body live the life it deserves without pain, or am I making my life worse by letting a substance take over my brain. Someone help me figure out the difference.

I don't feel anything anymore for anyone new. It's like everyone before these I still love, everyone during are just people I see when I take the drug.

I don't know what to do anymore. I can't believe I'm telling anyone this. I feel kinda sick and selfish even thinking about it.

I don't know who to talk to, I don't know what to do.

I'm sorry I chose you.

I never actually shared this poem with anyone until now. I was to embarrassed and afraid that someone might judge me and call me an addict, and with the reputation I had as a "good girl" because I don't drink, party or smoke, and the rumors about my family all being junkies and thieves, I couldn't tell anyone because no one would believe what I was doing, and why I was doing it. The notes in my phone became someone to talk to about how I was feeling and became my journal for everything I was trying to get out emotionally. The pain pills were not only taking my back pain away, they were starting to take all my pain away now- feelings being the main thing, my emotions began to feel paralyzed. I couldn't stop my experiment with them though, and at this point, I didn't really want too, I started to enjoy the feeling. I knew that I had to keep going because I needed more answers, and at this point my mind was playing so many tricks on me that I think that I felt like I was in way more pain than I really was, so the pills started becoming the answer to more than just physical pain - pain that I didn't know I still had within me. Pain pills started to become the answer, and that's when I started to really feel a deeper understanding of what addiction might feel like.

Ask yourself this, if there was a cure for every time you felt extreme pain, hopelessness, or were sad, would you of wished it could have been "cured" in that moment? Your answer is probably yes. Who wants to feel this way? Im guessing no one. An addicts only way to cope with their pain is by using again. Using becomes their answer because they have not been taught to deal with their pain any other way. And, if it wasn't so harmful to their bodies, this WOULD be the "cure," because they definitely do their job in the numbing department. Realistically, if you want to get technical, in a safe and controlled environment, drugs are the "answer" for everything, just in a pill form. Anxiety pills, depression pills, ADHD pills, pain pills, nerve pain pills, etc, etc, etc. There is literally a pill to help "cure" or manage almost everything we as humans feel. Therefore, when a struggling addict can't afford to see a doctor for what they are dealing with on the inside, aren't sure how to reach out for help, or are embarrassed about their addiction, it only makes sense that they would seek street drugs. An addict is searching for answers to try and take their pain, depression, anxiety or other mental illnesses they might be facing away, just like a "normal" functioning non-addict seeks help from a doctor when experiencing these illnesses, just with in a safer and more controlled environment.

An addict doesn't use just for pleasure. There is so much pain and suffering behind their use, and when using a drug can temporarily numb that pain, that is exactly what they want and think they need. For an outsider, you have got to learn to see their perspectives, instead of blaming others, blaming yourself and thinking that addicts are just disgusting terrible people who want to ruin their lives. There is a reason they use, and the only way they will stop, is if they find a BETTER reason than the drug, to stop. As a loved one of addiction, try and take a few minutes to understand their pain, switch the anger button off, and just listen to them without judgement. You might be surprised at what you hear, and how you feel after.

Chapter 9: My Feelings Just Disappeared

I started noticing my feelings fading for a lot of personal things pretty quickly with in my journey. My feelings just disappeared. When I had first moved to Las Vegas, I was sad every day. I would call my mom and grandma all the time saying how much I missed them and that I wanted to come home because everyone there was all about their money and was so rude. This depression phase changed pretty quickly. After a few months, I was starting to get texts from my mom asking if I still loved her because I wasn't reaching out as much anymore. Anything that was bothering me, or any pain physically and mentally that I had felt was always "cured" with the pills. It was crippling.

Anyone who would try and get close to me while I was there, I would push away because it felt weird to be around new people. And, if I wanted to go be around someone, the only way I could is if I was already on the pain pills. They were turning me so cold, I would hang out with a guy and he would tell me I acted just like him. He would say things like "you sound just like a man" because I would warn anyone who I spent time with to not like me, to not catch feelings for me, and would straight up tell them that I wasn't going to like them back, so there was really no point in hanging out. The crazy thing is, I really think I felt that way before the pills too (about hanging out with guys) but I just never had enough courage to tell people how I really felt. I didn't want to be close to anyone anymore. Other people, especially men made me feel so uncomfortable. I couldn't form a feeling of any sort, for anyone. I didn't care what they did, or what they said to me, I would just laugh in their face and say "okay." The word "okay," and "sorry" became my response to pretty much everything. I was lifeless at times.

The sad part is, today, I still find myself doing and feeling this way often. The pain pills definitely made this part of my life a little easier for me to not care, which I do miss. There are times I feel small spurts of what could maybe be feelings for someone now, but I'd be lying if I said I really cared that much. And maybe deep down I really do, but I can't see it yet, or feel it. Maybe because I am so afraid to ever feel what I felt before, or to lose someone again. It makes me feel like such a bad person. No one deserves to be treated that way.

Before the pills, I think I cared a little for men, but I never really felt like I was capable of loving a man how they deserved to be loved, even with my ex who I loved more than anything, I was still pretty cold to him at times. Maybe this stems from the feeling of thinking that a man would never really love me, not forever at least, because my dad didn't. This is something I probably will always struggle with and is my biggest downfall. At least when I was on the pills, they helped me kind of show my real feelings without feeling bad about how I felt, because when I would make someone sad, I felt nothing. Which is exactly what opioids are supposed to do for you - mask the pain, and to look back at my experience, they were doing just that, without me even realizing it.

I still struggle tremendously today with what feels real towards the person I am seeing, and what I am faking, and I do not take pills anymore. I do think that the pills still partially play apart in trying to distinguish the difference of what's real or not, even though it has been 2 months now since I've had one. I have no idea if this is normal or if this will always be how I am now. I do know that it makes me feel pretty bad, mostly because I wish I cared more not only about his feelings, but about my own. At the same time, feeling bad about how I feel, is still a feeling, even if it's not the right one, so it's something at least, right? Anyway, sorry for the rambling on, I just wanted to give you perspective of what drugs can do to a persons mind, such as my own, sorry for the rambling on, I just thought I would share how pills were affecting my mind at the time.

Chapter 10: Am I Still The Same Person

During my one year experiment, I began to seclude myself so much from everyone else that it started to feel normal to be alone. I would feel uncomfortable being around anyone else, unless I was already on pills. The pills gave me the confidence that I had lacked for so many years due to the embarrassment of my condition. They made me feel pretty, they made me feel free, they made me forget my insecurities and most importantly, they made me forget my physical pain. So, in my head, they were doing everything I wished I could feel without them, and that I had been longing for, for so long, that was taken from me due to life long physical pain.

> It's 3:00 am. I'm laying here with my eyes wide open. I'm broken.
>
> I never sleep anymore.
>
> I feel like I am kind of getting my mind back a little more everyday though, but ironically, today is not one of those days.
>
> My heart is pounding, but there is no pulse. I can see, but there is no light. I can hear, but there is no sound.
>
> Am I still the same person. I barely recognize myself. My mind wont let me speak any words. I've been forced to just write everything out, I guess that's why I'm writing this book.

Am I still the same person? I am screaming but no one can hear me. I am lost in the coldest woods. I wish someone would find me. I can't feel anything.

It's 4 am now. I'm still laying here. My mind went blank for awhile. Unpleasant memories surrounding my mind, my body feels heavy, I'm running out of time. I wish my mind could be steady, I am ready.

I don't have to look around to see darkness.

It's already submerged itself with in me. Where are my thoughts going. Keep looking for me.

I think I am getting tired. I'm going to close my eyes now. I hope to find myself when I come down.

The most concerning part about this poem is that I wrote it during a time that I was not on pills. It has been almost 3 months since I last had a pain pill. I have thought about them every single day since. My body physically needs them so badly. I ache so much with out them, and suffer almost everyday because of severe pain. But, I am aware that not only did the pain pills change who I was while I was on them, they have slightly changed who I am now. I try so hard to remember who I was before these, to remember a feeling I used to feel, but my feelings just seem to lay dormant, locked in a safe somewhere. I can feel them coming back slowly though.

I do not know if I will ever be the same person after this experience. There are days when I feel hope, and almost feel something, but it's not the same. Not yet at least. I know a lot of my emotional pain has to do with the fact that I was diagnosed with a rare disorder, and pain pills might be the only thing that will ever help, but now I know that I can't rely on them, even though I may have to some day. To think, I only did this for a year, I can't imagine how I would feel after years and years of use. I was only taking 4-6 pills a day. What's deranged is that no matter how hard I try, and no matter how much I know how poisonous these drugs can be to someones' body, my brain and body still wants them. I knew going into this experiment that I would never get addicted mentally, well at least that's what I told myself. I am, and always have been in control of every decision I make, every action I take, which is why I knew I could control this situation and always will be able to. I am the strongest person I know. I can do something and never do it again. I can eat something I love and if someone told me not to eat it again, I wouldn't. But, let me tell you this, and read this LOUDLY, when an addict tells you how hard it is to stop, please believe them, because I do now, not everyone is me and has my strength and willpower, I am just lucky to be strong minded enough to never cross that line, nor do I ever want to.

Willpower is one of the hardest things to control as humans. The only, and I mean the ONLY reason I will never take pain pills in excess again is because I now know how it affects who I am mentally and physically, and because what it's done to my family, not because I don't want to take them, because I do, and I would if they weren't so harmful to me mentally. I would take them everyday, they are the only thing that makes my body feel okay. But, regardless of my own willpower, I wasn't going to stop for anyone but myself, and frankly, I've had to learn the hard way that this is the case for all drug users. They will stop when THEY want to, not when you want them to.

I have no idea how long these affects will last, or how long I will continue to think about them, but I do believe the saying once an addict, always an addict because if the situation presented itself, I completely understand now why it would be so easy for the person to choose the drug again. It's definitely a craving that is so hard to explain, it's almost like your body can remember the feeling even when you aren't on them, and your brain gives you a small dose of it from your memory bank, and then begs you to feel that way again. It's sad. It's sickening. Drugs are so powerful. DON'T DO DRUGS, and don't do what I did to find answers, ever.

I came back to this section to re-read what I wrote before sending it off to publishers who were interested in my book, and it actually shocked me to read what I wrote. I let someone read parts of my book and their first initial response was "so you were an addict" and my answer for anyone who is thinking that or questioning that, will always be no, and I never will be, and I can confidently say that with no hesitation. I tried to feel that urge my brother and cousin, and other loved ones have talked about, I tried to cross that line. But, I literally never could. My mind, body, soul and self worth would not allow me to. Because I have mastered the part of self love and self discipline with in me, and when or if you ever do the same, you will understand exactly what I mean. When you really love yourself, your body and mind will not allow you to do certain things. I am still human, and yes, I still get sad and have negative thoughts from time to time, but, as of lately, I have learned how to deal with those thoughts through patience and love for myself, and everyday my mind grows stronger. Believe me, I wanted to try and feel what an addict feels, I wanted to experience it and understand it, but my experiment only took me so far, far enough to write a book and share it with you I suppose.

I still get prescribed pain pills today for my chronic disease, and I most likely will for the rest of my life, unless someone comes up with a cure for Ehlers- Danlos Syndrome. Not once have I ever taken over a certain amount, and I've literally never wanted to. I am incapable of becoming an addict, this is very possible for anyone out there doubting that. A strong mind can overcome anything in this world. I hope whoever is reading this understands that drugs are in fact a choice at first, and always will be, and unless you learn to love yourself in all the right ways, drugs will take over your mind, body and soul and THEY will become YOUR disease, until you change your mental state.

Chapter 11: My Own Story

To get a real sense of where I ended up, first you need to understand where I came from. I guess this is what you have all been waiting for. Well, here you go.

I was 10 years old the very first time I saw someone use hard drugs. It was a 50 year old, unemployed black man with ripped jeans and holes all over his shirt. He was sitting in the front seat of his van, which was also his home, with a blow up doll in the front seat with him who he called his girlfriend. I was sitting in the back seat on his tore up leather cushion with my two brothers and uncle, when he laid out a line of white powder on his dash board. He hesitantly looked back at all 4 of us and said " don't tell your mom," turned back around and snorted it with a one dollar bill that had looked so old and was so perfectly rolled, that it's only purpose was exactly what it was being used for. That 50 year old man was my grandpa.

I guess you can say I've never really told "my story" to anyone, not even the people I love most in this world – but, I think it's finally time to explain why I've struggled with understanding addiction for so long, and how I allowed it to it take over my life before making my own changes.

Through out my journey while writing this book, everyone I talked to was so open about their story, that I knew it would only be fair if I was too. I'm obviously not going to tell you guys everything because a lot of my life is embarrassing, and it would take up hundreds of pages, so I'll spare some of the details. I'm probably going to be pretty terrible at expressing my own story because I've tried to permanently suppress so many of these feelings forever, that now they are like flowers that haven't been watered in 3 weeks and that haven't seen the light of day in months. So bare with me, here goes nothing.

For so many years, I thought that this would always be how I lived, and that the things I saw and went through in my life were normal for every young kid my age. I grew up around so many people whose lives were limited by their own lack of knowledge and education. My dad only made it through 9th grade, and my mom graduated high-school. No one on my dads side made it past high-school and most of them never even graduated, either. I guess statistically I was never supposed to make it out.

When I finally started to realize how dysfunctional and fucked up my family really was, I began to harbor so many hateful feelings towards my family members for their lifestyle choices. As the years went on, I began to keep everything a secret from everyone I knew because in my head everyone had their own problems, and I never wanted to use my life as an excuse for my failures, or for my success, well, and because it was embarrassing as fuck that no one knew who my dad was and that my family members we junkies. I told myself I would never be a victim of my circumstances and that someone somewhere else was always going to have it worse than me, so I just kept my life as private as possible.

It's hard to even know where to start when it comes to telling my story. I miss who I'll never really know, because I can't remember a time that some of the people closest to me were ever even clean from drugs. I had already lost so many people mentally to addiction that I was able to somehow still be okay with the lifestyle as I got older because it was so normal with in my family, and it wasn't until I physically lost one of my friends to addiction, that finally gave me the wake up call mentally that I needed. After that, a lot changed for me and how I viewed almost every thing in my life. This was the beginning of me learning to redirect my thought process into trying to purely understand addiction from a different perspective with an open heart. Instead of always being against drugs and hating everything involved with them, and hiding my feelings about it, I chose to accept that part of my life and move forward because

I learned that no matter what I did or said, I could not change who my family was, and what they were doing. Losing someone permanently made me realize how short life was, and that at any point, I could lose someone else. This is when my hate towards addiction shifted my own attitude by realizing that there was no point of always being mad at my loved ones anymore because it was never going to change them, it was only changing me. I had to separate the two, for me, love and addiction could no longer be placed in the same category. I had to learn to detach the fact that just because my family were addicts, didn't mean they deserved more, or less love from me, and it didn't mean they were a bad person, either.

As an outsider of addiction, I had to learn to love them through a different lens, one with a more clear picture on my own end. I knew I could not change what has already happened, and I could not predict the future, either, but, one thing I could do was love them unconditionally, change my own state of mind, and continue to care for them, even if it was from a distance.

When I was young, I became so accustomed to not being who I really was. I never wanted to be anything like my family. I was so humiliated for so long that I had family members who were addicts, thieves, uneducated, and that I was poor, that I let it consume my own life and my own feelings towards the people I loved for years. I had allowed other peoples' perception of my family to affect my own love and understanding for them, and I let it ruin my relationships with people I cared for, who just needed my support.

I remember my friends parents wouldn't allow them to come over to my house because of my families past, and because who my mom was dating at the time. There were times that they would sneak over anyway, and their parents would literally circle my block checking to see if they were over at my house. They would drive around and around for literally an hour. It was so embarrassing. (F them by the way because I am good ass person, but whatever, I hope they read this and feel dumb). Anyway, as a young woman, because of other people's impression of me, based off of my families misfortunes, I found myself always lying and pretending to be who I wasn't. All my friends lived normal lives and had a mom and a dad, I just wanted to feel normal and be like them, even if it was for pretend. I hid what went on behind closed doors in my real life, and my real feelings from everyone because everyone had already assumed that I was like the rest of my family anyway before even giving me a chance. There were times I would go to softball tournaments and my coaches would come into my room and check my clothes bag to see if I stole anything from the stores they took us to, or to see if I had brought alcohol with me. I was being placed in a box by everyone around me, and because of it, I became so sheltered and so resentful towards my family. I never felt good enough for anyone, no matter how hard I tried to fake it. No matter what I did or what I accomplished, it never took away who my family was and how people thought about us, it was never enough to take my real identity away.

My insecurities about who I was and what I could turn into started to affect me more and more as I got older - I became so fearful that my potential would always be limited because of my circumstances. The worst part about it all was that because of the way I looked, people on the outside thought I lived this glamorous life and had everything so easily. And, don't get me wrong, sure I was still popular because I was pretty, and dated professional athletes and millionaires blah, blah, but it still never took away where I came from and how I felt about myself, or who my family was. Money, fame, attention, those were all temporary fixes for me. I could feel myself losing control the more I was not living up to what others' perception of me was. On top of that, everyone in my family looked up to me, if they needed an answer, I had to be there with one, I never had anyone that I could reach out to. The words "I'm fine" became permanent answers for every kind of question. I felt like I could not live my true life.

Over time, my brother's addiction got so bad that I often felt like I was the parent to my mom, often consoling her and letting her know everything would be okay. I had to learn to shut off my own feelings so I could stay strong for her, leaving me emotionally masked and damaged at a really young age. I didn't know who to talk to, and I didn't know how to talk to anyone because there was never time for my own problems. I felt like I was only there to help everyone else in my family, I had to carry my family's torch, knowing if I were to ever let the flame go out that we would have nothing left. I had to learn to turn my feelings off, I had to learn to not show emotion because if I did, who else was going to be strong for my family. I turned into a stone cold savage over time let me tell you. I began to learn how to compartmentalize every thought and feeling I ever had, making it easier for me to mentally survive. I got so good at hiding my real feelings, that even when I was alone, and no one was around, I didn't even show my feelings to myself because I literally didn't know how to.

Over the years, the more I disconnected myself from that identity, a lot of people started telling me how weird I was, how in my own world I was, and how they didn't understand why I preferred to be alone. A lot of my friends and family never understood why I didn't like to be in relationships and why men made me uncomfortable. But, none of them have seen or felt what I felt, and it seemed like every man I ever loved, loved drugs more. On top of that, when you have a "dad" that wants nothing to do with you, and I mean nothing, it makes you feel pretty worthless. And, when your entire life is surrounded by drugs, being alone and not having to deal with that lifestyle for five minutes, feels pretty damn good. Truthfully, for so long, and even until this day, I felt that if my dad doesn't even love me, how could another man ever love me.

The only memories I have of my dad stay stuck in my head, they swarm round and round like a dangerous whirlpool. I've never said the word dad out loud. How weird is that. If somehow he ever reads this, I'll probably feel pretty bad about it, which I don't know how I could still love him when he doesn't feel the same. But, fuck it, I'm going to tell you a little bit about the man they call my dad.

I have five memories of the man that made me. Five. That's because there weren't really many other times that I saw him because he was either in prison for identity theft and possession and probably some sort of sex trafficking shit, too. But, the main reason was because he just didn't want to see me. One time when I was 9, he randomly came to visit me and my brother, and my mom had just got me McDonalds. I'll never forget the disgust on his face when he saw me eating that chicken sandwich. He looked at me and told me how ugly I was getting, and told my mom to take the food out of my hand because I was getting too fat, and to stop feeding me after 5pm. HAHAHA. Wow, writing that just made me super angry.

Another memory I have of him is when I was 12, he brought me into his room and showed me his escort, and told me this is how women should look, and then later that day took my cousin and I to the boys and girls club so he could "run errands," but he never showed up to pick us up. We walked home at 10pm that night, alone.

Another memory I have of him was when I was 17. I walked into the gym to watch my cousins play basketball and he happened to be there. I was wearing a crop top (which I always wear) and will never forget the way he looked at me. An uneasy feeling to say the least. I couldn't tell if he was repulsed, angry, or thought his own daughter looked good (I hope not the last one). All he kept saying out loud to everyone around is "why the fuck are you wearing something like that, you're my daughter?"

The fourth memory I have of him was when I was 19. He randomly showed up at one of my softball games and waved at me. I was the first one to bat, and I hit a home run the first pitch. When I looked into the stands to find him after the first inning, he was gone. I did just enough for him to tell people about me, but, I wasn't good enough for him to stay the whole game and say hi to me after.

The last memory I have of him happened pretty recently actually. He's never called me on my birthday or any holiday, but for some reason he randomly got a hold of me during Christmas time to tell me he had some gifts for me. It was pretty weird and unexpected. When I went over there, he just kept giving me shit. Clothes, backpacks, perfume, coats, shoes. His bedroom looked like a Macy's during the holidays, it was a sight to see that's for sure. Now don't get me wrong, I was very appreciative because he had never given me anything before, and even though I knew where he got it all, I still was going to take that shit, with the sensors strapped on them and all. HAHA. Anyway, while I was there, I asked why he had all the medicine behind him and he told me he recently was told that he had high blood pressure and diabetes. Then he persisted on taking his blood pressure in front of me to show me his little machine the doctors gave him, and his fucking blood pressure was literally 190/126. I said holy shit that's high! He told me "ya I guess I should stop using heroin or there's no point in me taking all this medicine." That was the first time he ever admitted to me that he was an addict, even though he has been one since he was 16.

Anyway, enough about that, my point is drugs took my dad away before I even knew who he was. I truly don't think he even knows how to have a relationship with people, the only one he has with my brother is when they use together and even then, it's almost like he gives it to him so he can feel like he is better than him. That's the man that made me. Unfortunately, I know that my dad kicked my mom in the stomach and gave her an abortion so she couldn't have a second kid, then a few months later got her pregnant again with me. I can't help to think that maybe that's why he doesn't like me, he wasn't able to kill me this time.

I guess I'll never know if he is sorry for what he's said to me over the years, or if he even cares that he has negatively affected my life. He has made it very hard for me to love or trust any man, and I know that I should talk to someone about it, or shit maybe I should get the nerve to ask him why he didn't want anything to do with me and my brother. I guess I am asking him now right. So, there ya go, "Dad," if you ever read this, you should know the truth. Your actions and absence has really affected me, even if I pretended it never did. I'm sorry I only had the courage to say all this to you through writing, and no matter what has happened, I still forgive you and love you.

For sooooo long I was so resentful towards my brother. He made everything in my life so much harder than it needed to be, and as a young girl, I just wanted to be normal and fit in. But, no, because of his addiction, we stood out like a white person at a black families family reunion. I was always so mad at him because in my head, he was going through the same issue I was with the feelings towards our dad, and if I could be okay, then he should of been okay too. That was so wrong of me to think this way, and I hope he knows how sorry I am if I ever made him feel less, or unworthy. He is the main reason I am writing this book. I love my brother so much, and when I was younger, all I ever wanted was to be just like him. If he liked a team, I liked it too. If he played a sport, I wanted to play to, and be on his team. He was so funny and so outgoing when he was young and clean, that I'm pretty sure I am the girl version of him now, and if he ever got clean again we would probably be just alike. Before I started to understand addiction, I hated how our relationship was developing. I didn't ever want to be around him. Every excuse he made, every lie he told, every time he would go back to jail, it just pushed me further away from him because I was disgusted with his behavior and truly believed he should just be able to quit. My brother turned into a bonafide hustler. And the crazy thing is, he knew how to be from such a young age. He would sell the food stamp cards we got, he would trade his clothes, cigarettes, rake peoples lawns and even collect cans just to get high and earn some money. He was so good at it, and that's what made it so easy for him to keep using. For so long I blamed him for my ex's drug use, I blamed him for why we had to move all the time, I blamed him for why my older brother was distant from the family, I blamed him for my moms sadness, and I blamed him for being unhappy myself. I learned so much through out my brothers addiction, some good things, and some bad things. I am so lucky that nothing bad ever happened to him during the time that I treated him like an outsider and blamed him for my own unhappiness. I did not know how to cope with my own feelings, and it was always easier to just blame him. Today, I still am very sad that my brother is an addict, but our relationship is so much stronger because I learned to take a step back, take responsibility for my own well-being and learned to love him from a different perspective. I love you brother, and I will always be here for you, when, or if you ever turn your life around, I will always still love you the same.

I am, and alway will be grateful for my mom. She was a single parent who worked 2-3 jobs sometimes to support my family and try and give us the most normal life she knew how. She is the best person I know, and nothing will ever take that away from her. But, a lot of my own pain developed from seeing what shes been through and not being able to stop it, or help her. I always wanted her to feel good about herself because of everything she had been through, so I never judged her about the men she dated, and always just supported her decisions. But, when you see your mom being beaten almost to death, and food and shoes being thrown at her, and men cheating on her, you can't help but to harbor your feelings deep inside. I remember one time I caught one of my moms boyfriends cheating on her, and I instantly felt a rush of sickness go over my entire body. This man months before this had asked my mom to marry him, I didn't want to break her heart. Not again. I found myself always stuck in the middle, I just wanted my mom to be happy. A few of her boyfriends would privately message me telling me how good I looked, and would always say inappropriate things to me when my mom wasn't around. When I was really young, I remember I would wake up and see the man she was dating at the time standing over my bed. This is the same guy that blacked my moms eyes and broke her nose right in front of me. To this day, I don't feel comfortable around white men (weirdly this was the only white man my mom ever dated), and I don't really know why, or if I ever will feel comfortable around them. But, because of everything my mom did for me, I never could tell her this kind of stuff, not because she wouldn't believe me (because trust me if I told her this at the time she probably would be in jail for murder) but because I hated seeing her hurt, and didn't want to maker her think that she had chosen another piece of shit man. I didn't want her to think it was my fault, and I just wanted one of her relationships to work out so she could be happy again. I still to this day have no idea how she is so strong and how she managed to raise us through all the bullshit, and still is such a good person after everything she went though. YOU are the real MVP momma girl.

Anyway, like everyone else, we all have our secrets and reasons for why we do what we do. My secrets and life led me to wanting to understand addiction on a deeper level. I used to harbor so much tension towards my mom for always allowing men to come into our house and for allowing my brother to continue using and enabling him, but, she wasn't going to give up on her son and my brother wasn't going to stop using, so allowing it to consume MY life wasn't worth it anymore. I had to control what I could, and the only thing I had power over, was my own mind and feelings.

If I could give my reader one piece of important advice, I would say to just love your family no matter what, because life is to short not to. Now, that doesn't mean enable them, that doesn't mean let them control you, and it doesn't mean you have to agree with what they are doing. But, as someone who has experienced every side to the this battle now, the best thing I ever did for myself was to love my family from a distance, and instead focus only on what

I could control. Learn to love them for who they are, stop trying to fix every-thing, and just be there for them mentally if they need you, before it's too late.

To go forward a bit. When Zach died, this was the moment I mentally changed who I was, and how I would now view life. I knew everything I did in the past, had to change. I HAD to redirect my thought process if I was ever going to get my own life back. My coping skills, behaviors, mind set, and love for myself became my only focus in gaining my purpose back. Below, I will share a poem with you that I wrote for Zach after he died.

" Wassup love"

He sent me this message on the 9th of September, it'll sit in my
phone forever. God, help me to remember.
Why didn't I remember to write him back?
I can't get this shit off my mind.
A week later he was gone, why didn't I give him my time?
Zach text me again! please just tell me you're fine.
It gets harder to breathe knowing what you left behind.
Please just tell me they're lyin
2 brothers, nephews, friendships, family your poetry.
I can't help to think the reason you texted me was to reach out to me.
Lives lived on similar paths, Memories fucking up our heads trying
to forget our pasts.
Seen things and heard things nobody can mask.
But why God have to take you so fast?
Pain won this time and now my heart hurts everyday.
I wish you coulda known in time that pain fades away.
Sometimes I wish we coulda traded places for the day.
I wish I could have looked inside your mind to know what was caus-
ing you so much pain.
Theres no words to describe the feelings that remain.

You're gone, and things will never be the same.

Please know your existence will never fade.

*You inspired your friends to always be brave, you stepped outside of
the game.*

You made us all know your name.

Zach Tackwell.

Yes, say his name. a genius, a poet, meant for center stage.

We all love you zach, that will never change.

I miss you. I promise to continue being a better friend, companion, daughter, sister, niece, auntie, and grand daughter because of you. Thank you for inspiring me to be different.

For so long, I had allowed my mind to always be bigger than myself. I didn't know how to control my emotions towards the ones I loved and it wasn't only negatively affecting my personal relationships, it was affecting my own life to the point where I had no control. Before finding who I really was, trying to accomplish what my mind wanted, was often crippling. I fought with myself everyday with what I wanted and what I needed, and it left me stuck in a place I often didn't know how to get out of. For years, I allowed my insecurities of my past to control my outcomes, but the older I got, the stronger minded I became. I was able to take my own mistakes that I made with my loved ones addiction, and learn to cope with my own feelings towards it in a way that opened up my heart and eyes to the bigger picture.

Addiction will always play a part in my life. The reality is, my family will always struggle with addiction, but I have the strength now to be who I really am, and do what I really want, and it's such a rewarding and freeing feeling. Addiction can negatively affect so many people, not just the addict, and I am so grateful that I took the time to understand it more clearly. I have prospered in so many ways because of it. I hope that this book helps you find your own strength, and that it gives you the answers you have been searching for as well.

Chapter 12: Self Love vs. Self Discipline

SELF LOVE IS SELF DISCIPLINE. Let me say that one more time so it sticks like gorilla glue to your head. Self love IS self discipline. I truly believe that learning to discipline your own behaviors with mindful practice, is the most important characteristic one can have. Mastering this ability can open up so many doors for someone who wonders why they continue to come up short in specific areas of their lives, and do not know how to redirect their emotions and thoughts into actions that are more consistent, beneficial, and positive to their lifestyles. Learning to obtain self discipline by harnessing your self love, can change your thought process, your behaviors, your routines, and most importantly, it can change your outcomes. Once you have learned to do this daily, and can possess this skill without thinking about it, you will be capable of understanding your own feelings in ways that will make life so much smoother for you. Self discipline revolves around self love!

Sadly, these two traits – self love and self discipline, are both what a drug user lacks most. Drug users ultimately know that drugs are bad for them, but they are not capable of registering the part of them that controls self discipline, due to the inadequacy of self love they have developed for themselves over time. In return, because they are incapable of exhibiting self love from within, to tell their mind to stop their negative behaviors, they form the same patterns, creating the same results repeatedly, because they fall short in these two areas that allows them to make positive choices routinely.

When someone has not yet learned to register the part of them that contains self love, they lack the part of them that is able to say no to anything that is harmful to their over all wellbeing. For example, ACTUALLY possessing self discipline is when you see a drug at a party and everyone else is doing it, and sure you might want to do it to, but the SELF LOVE in you is telling you "hey that's not good for you, you probably shouldn't do that," thus, you DON'T do it, because self discipline comes from your own self love, and anyone who possesses self love, loves who they are too much to hurt their "healthy self." As I mentioned above, when you lack these characteristics; which most addicts do, incidents that pop up that are bad for you, that can hurt you, and that you wouldn't normally do in a good and healthy state of mind, don't even get thought about for a second, you just do them thinking there are no consequences because you haven't manifested the part of you that controls self love and self discipline. This is why learning to love who you are is the most important trait anyone can have, in any form, and in any situation. Once you love yourself fully, you are capable of having and controlling self discipline, over anything else. Self love IS self discipline and grasping ahold onto these two monumental traits, might just be the answer you have been searching for.

I can't end with just that. I need you guys to really soak this information in. This chapter is extremely important for every one of you who picked up my book, and I want all of my readers to benefit from this chapter because believe me, if you can grasp a hold of these two characteristics, and truly make positive steps towards them everyday, you WILL become a happier human being. I am 99 percent sure that self love and self discipline are the keys to happiness and productivity.

Let me begin by telling you how and why. First and foremost, being proud of the way you live should be your ultimate goal every single day that you open up those crusty eyes of yours in the morning. Making smart and thoughtful decisions that bring about long term peace to your mind, and long term wellness to your body, should be the guiding principles of your everyday actions.

But, first, you have to learn the difference between the healthy, and the unhealthy version of you before anything else. Here's how.

To do this successfully, you have start by practicing to talk back to your unhealthy self - the part of you that lacks self esteem and self love, every time you feel confused, lost, or are questioning your behaviors, even if at first you don't truly believe what you're saying back to yourself holds true. It takes practice, patience, and responsibility to create a repertoire of healthy responses, so that you're more readily prepared to combat your unhealthy self - the self the lacks self love. You can begin this journey by coming up with specific statements to say back to yourself when you are feeling doubtful, that are unique to your own situation. Practicing these type of skills will eventually becomes routines, that will help to feed the healthy version of your mind, body and soul. The ultimate goal is to not get rid of your unhealthy self - but to learn from it, discover what it's doing for you, and by taking the knowledge and understanding of moments you notice yourself falling back into bad habits, and instead learning to turn them into ways that strengthen your self love and self discipline, so that eventually you are able to replace and take over your unhealthy thoughts, with new healthy and effective ones.

Those who have yet to master these two traits, are unaware that they even have two versions of themselves – the healthy version that is capable of obtaining self love and self discipline, and the unhealthy version – the side of you who has completely different feelings, thoughts and behaviors than your healthy self. It's your unhealthy self that will talk you into behaviors such as drug use, unprotected sex, violence, etc. This must change if success, happiness and productivity is something you crave in life.

Don't feel overwhelmed, this kind of change doesn't just happen over night. You can start this new journey of self love by installing these characteristics into your mind, and into your habits a little more every day, so that doing so will help you create a new sense of pride that comes from doing the right things. It all begins with educating your mind to dictate your outcomes, but still listening to your inner voice by learning to distinguish the difference between your healthy and unhealthy thoughts. Changing the way we act and think can only happen by replacing one bad habit with a good one, and by learning to adjust our thoughts into positive behaviors, that will benefit you for long term purposes.

So why should this matter to you, and what should you expect to start to happen to you when you begin to see changes in yourself for the better? Well, when your self discipline becomes your self love, you get up early because you want to, you cook because you feel like cooking, you exercise because it feels good, you join a class because you want to learn more, and, when you need more sleep, you let yourself without feeling bad about it because self love also means self acceptance. Gaining control over these two traits also helps boost confidence, it allows you to be in control of yourself, your emotions, your moods, and most importantly, it effects how you see yourself internally knowing you are now in control. Loving yourself first before anything else is YOUR ticket to happiness, so get on the damn train and get your life back! You are worth it!

Chapter 13: The 5 Stages of Change

There are 5 stages that people go through while trying to break a bad habit. Unfortunately, the majority of them get stuck somewhere in the middle phase, without ever fully reaching the final stage. The first stage is the pre-contemplation stage. During this process, people do not intend to take action in the foreseeable future, and frankly just don't have much interest in actually changing. The next stage is the contemplation stage. During this phase, people begin to prepare themselves by making positive strides towards shifting their behaviors to see positive outcomes with in 6 months or so, but don't know how to start or what to do. Then comes the preparation stage. Preparation stage is a lot like the contemplation stage, people begin to make small adjustments with their frame of mind, they are getting ready to change, and they aim to take action in the near future. After this, comes the action stage. In this period, people have taken specific steps within their lifestyle to help maintain quitting their bad habit. Last, comes the maintenance stage. During this process, people have made specific and positive reinforcements in their life that keeps them from doing the same thing recurrently, and indulge their focus on ways to prevent relapse.

These 5 stages occur in almost any scenario that prevents people from living a better quality of life. With in these steps, excuses, relapses, and negativity towards their goals often hinder the person from completing each step. One major reason why people get trapped in a limbo usually between stages 1 through 3 is because they are not seeing concrete results fast enough, most often because they are doubtful that they can actually fully overcome their struggle. This occurs when they have tried to change multiple times and are producing little to no results, so they convince themselves that it is impossible for them to have success. These 5 stages control anyone who is trying to transform their lifestyle.

Think about ALL the times you may have tried to make a change in your own life, and how many times you failed at it. For example, I'm sure most of you have tried every single fad diet ever known to man, and at first you thought to yourself "yes, I want to change!" Then, you started your diet (probably on a Monday) and you started eating healthy, maybe even started working out a little bit more, and as the days went on you started feeling pretty good about yourself. A few weeks, or maybe a even a month goes by and you have made it all the way to the action stage without going back to your old ways. 2 months fly by and BOOM, you hit a wall and you stop seeing the same results as the first month on the scale, and on your body. This is where regression starts to take over your confidence and desire to keep going. So, instead of being patient and hopeful, and realizing that you in fact are still making progress, you start making less trips to the gym, and you start catching yourself saying things like well "F it I'm not losing anymore weight so I might as well eat bad," creating a negative outlook towards something that is only meant to be positive. You begin to allow your emotions to make you temporarily quit, causing you to be stuck in the limbo stage. This is the most common reason why people stay content with their lives because they don't want to put the extra work in. I used to let this happen to me multiple times because for years, I wasn't really ready to change my mindset, or my behaviors for the long run because I didn't know how. I had to understand that real change that didn't include detailed plans and solutions, was like a builder trying to build a house without blueprints. This is why it's so important to focus on ways to prevent from going back to your old habits, by incorporating detailed plans that involve more permanent solutions for long term success. Maintaining your overall goal is JUST as important as the steps you take to get there.

For an addict, this is exactly how and why relapses occur. Relapses happen in all types of situations that involve living healthier because people do not want to maintain their progress if they are not seeing or feeling the results of what they believed or thought they would feel. Just like you with all your yo-yo diets, you quit because of no results, people will stop their addiction when they are ready to, and on their own terms when they feel they are ready. No one can force you to stop smoking, to eat better, or to go to the gym, you have to want to change, and you have to continue to reach milestones through your entire journey in order to maintain that change to be successful.

Changing a bad habit can be overwhelming and demoralizing, think about how easier said than done, quitting drugs might be. Therefore, Instead of trying to control someone else's drug use by putting them down, or by trying to change them, understand that changing takes time, and maybe shift your focus more on providing them with positivity and reassurance that change IS in fact possible, because they could be completely unaware that you still care for them. Remember any form of recovery or change is not a linear process, every one of you will experience ups and downs, stalls, slips and maybe even relapses in your journey. The important piece to maintaining change is to keep trying, never give up too soon, learn to create new structure within your life and keep your motivation strong!

Now that you see how being negative does nothing for you or someone you are trying to help, changing your intentions, having a more in depth understanding of addiction, and implementing your own actions towards someone's struggle has to replace your current actions, if you want to make your own life better. The most important thing you can do for an addict who is stuck in these five stages is providing them with positive feedback and reinforcement through their entire process. If a user decides that they even want to take these steps, it shows strides in the right direction, but like with any positive change, getting there can take time and real effort. Be sure to encourage them, help them through it, and be strong within your own morals and rules during this process, if you do decide you want to be apart of it. The rest is left up to them, and them only. Quitting something you have done for so long, isn't going to be easy to do, and doesn't just magically vanish overnight.

With any bad habit- over eating, not going to the gym, smoking cigarettes, it takes time and discipline to really see success in changing what you are used to doing. If changing were so easy, everyone would do it and everyone would be healthy, but it's clearly not that simple. Developing a real change in your own attitude towards addiction is going to take patience, understanding and real effort on your end day in and day out, just like your loved ones battle with addiction, it takes will, desire and action to want to turn your negative habit, into something positive. You can do this!

Chapter 14: From Their Own Mouths

"The lucky ones are those who overdose and die from heroin when they are young"

~ *Anonymous*

I knew this book wouldn't be complete without the help of others. I wanted to get as many people as I could to participate and tell me their story about how addiction has affected their lives to show all different types of perspectives. At first, when I reached out, I was blown away by the amount of people who wanted to help me with this section of my book. I posted on Facebook saying I was writing a book about the perspectives of an addict and how to better understand this lifestyle, and I had tons of people privately messaging me saying they would love to help and be apart of this, and even thanking me for doing what I was doing. For those who did help, it was almost like they had all been wanting to talk about it for years with someone else who wouldn't judge them and who could relate, but were just to afraid to let it out. I knew some of them personally, and others I had never met in my life. Reading the responses from some of the people who I knew, was tough to say the least, and honestly very unexpected. It's so crazy what people go through that stays left unsaid. A lot of the people who reached out just wanted someone to listen to them, someone who wasn't going to make them feel bad about how they felt, and I think I became that person for them – it was comforting, but crazy and overwhelming at the same time. Some of their stories made me instantly tear up because so much of it was relatable, which continued to prove that addiction affects everyone and all walks of life, not just the addict.

As the responses started flowing in, dispiritedly a pattern seemed to arrive. A lot of people seemed really eager to help out, but then as soon as I would send the questions to them, their attitude towards it changed, and they seemed stand-offish. The majority of the people who did respond were loved ones of an addict, and they usually answered most of my questions with in a timely manner.

The most disappointing part through my writing process occurred when I would have people respond saying "I would love to help, I currently use, go ahead ask me anything" - but, as soon as I sent the questions over to them, poof, they disappeared, or they would say "never mind, I don't really have time for that." For this reason, my book was put on hold a little bit longer than I wanted it to be because I could not, and did not want to continue without hearing from this population.

Getting anyone to respond who was a current struggler of addiction was like pulling teeth. No one wanted to answer any of my questions and I had to continue asking the same people if they still were interested, usually getting left on "read." After a couple weeks of reaching out again, I did finally get a couple people to respond and answer a few of my questions at least, but, sadly not as many as I had hoped for.

Below I will be sharing some of their responses to some of the questions I conducted during their interviews, some of it is going to be shocking, while other answers are going to seem familiar and very interconnected. I hope that this section of my book helps you understand that you are not alone, and other people who are struggling with addiction or has a loved one who struggles, is going through some of the same pain you are. You are not alone, we are all in this together, and we all all searching for answers.

Questions and answers from loved ones of an addict:

Anonymous-

1. **If you could change one thing about your loved ones addiction, what would it be?**

The one thing I would change is that I would want them to be more capable of quitting, and that it could be easier for them to recover from addiction more easily.

I would have changed how deep he got into it so quickly.

If I could change one thing about my loved ones addiction it would be to make health care more affordable so they could afford to see a professional to get proper help.

I would change the loss of her motivation, often she has the right mind set to change and she has the insight to do so, but, because of the lack of motivation the change never lasts long enough to save her from this nightmare.

2. **Do you take it personal that your loved ones use, do you blame yourself?**

I do not take it personal for them using, I think that it's important to be there for a loved one who struggles, while keeping an open-mind.

I do not take blame for any of my loved ones using drugs, it was their own choice. I did take it personal, however, I didn't feel any blame while it was happening. I felt mad, that he didn't see his worth, that he didn't see his families worth to have him clean and honest.

I do take it personal at times that she uses. The reason I take it personal is because she misses out on a ton of things I need her present for. Birthdays, holidays, weddings- times that cannot be replaced.

3. What is one thing you wish you could understand more about addiction?

I really don't think it is to be understood. I've heard every excuse in the book and I just still don't understand it.

I wish that I could understand why they would even start using knowing exactly what it does to a persons' state of mind and know how addictive drugs and alcohol can be.

I wish that I could understand what that person feels and thinks to make them choose drugs. I would like to know what draws them in.

I wish that I could help addicts realize and know that they are worthy of a good life. That if they just put in the work and make the change they can deal with their pain and problems in a different way. That numbing the pain might be easier, but all it does is more damage than good in the long run.

One thing I wish I would have done is to not be so stubborn with my tough love approach. I didn't take the time to understand addiction or how hard the battle really was. I have never been addicted, so to me, it seemed like my brother should have just been able to quit and that he was just babying it. That wasn't the case, that wasn't the life he wanted. That wasn't the life he even realized he had gotten that far into until the end. I wish I would have been more educated before I judged.

4. Do you find yourself questioning your love for them?

I would never love anyone less because they were an addict. Alcohol has affected me personally, and now that I am a mom I don't drink around my kids. Not that it is a bad thing to have a drink, but I just don't want them to see me with one.

I never question my love. If anything I love them harder out of fear that they might not be around in the future.

I never questioned my love. I loved my brother more than anything in this entire world. He was always my role model, even in the darkest days. I loved that man with everything I had in me. It hurt like hell seeing him self destruct, but I loved him so much that I would rather him be here being a self destructing drug addict than the route he decided to take.

5. How has addiction affected you personally?

Unfortunately, I think that drugs will always affect me. It's something that is always in the back of my mind, most of my childhood was based around the drug lifestyle. But, oddly enough I am very proud of where I come from and love who I have become due to my past. I peeked under the bathroom floor when I was 5 years old and watched my dad stick a needle in his arm and that was the worst thing I've ever experienced. After that it went down hill. I was always hiding from probation officers, running from the FEDS, cops kicking down doors, finding needles and guns around the house at a very young age, having to watch my newborn sister when I was only 7 years old, there's so much more that I could probably write my own book on it. Iv'e had every odd stacked against me growing up, and still I prevailed and learned!

Addiction consumes my life, and I am not an addict. But, I live constantly in fear that I will get a call saying the worst. I have been robbed of time of time that should have been spent with my loved ones, I have been robbed of the relationship we once shared. Addiction stole my best friend from me.

My brother took his own life because he couldn't handle being a drug addict. He became everything he hated. Everything he never wanted to be. 7 months, it only took 7 months for heroin to ruin my families lives completely, forever.

6. How has addiction affected your loved ones?

In so many ways. There is constant fighting and bickering over wrongful doings. There is constant fear of losing our loved one, but we also have to set boundaries to keep ourselves safe and sane. We have spent sleepless nights in the hospital scared that this might be the time that she doesn't bounce back. We have spent several birthday's and holidays talking to her over the phone because she was in jail. We have seen and heard things that we never in a million years thought we would ever be dealing with. It has caused tension, stress and fighting throughout my family and it has completely tore my family apart.

Not only have I seen my brother physically deteriorate, I notice more and more that mentally he is not the same anymore, either. He has become someone I don't recognize anymore and lives in environments that are so unsanitary and disgusting that makes me sick to my stomach because when he's clean, he's a germaphobe.

7. Do you think addiction is a choice or a disease?

I don't think that there is a black and white answer to this question. I feel it's a little bit of both. While you choose to ultimately pick up that beer bottle, needle, or foil, a lot of those who suffer have mental illnesses that they are trying to self medicate.

I believe that addiction is both. Addiction is a choice chosen by the person, but on the other hand there is some addiction that has become a disease like drug addicted kids that were born into addictions. The ones that chose to taste, experiment and let curiosity get the best of them chose that addiction to consume them mentally and physically.

I think addiction is both a disease and a choice. They made the bad choice to start using at one point in time, but then it eventually becomes a sickness. A disease that takes over until they die, end up in prison, or eventually can make another choice to change. Even after an addict is clean, I feel that the disease never goes away. They are constantly dealing with triggers or relapses for the rest of their lives. But, just like someone with diabetes, you can learn to live with the disease and get by. An addict just has to be willing to put in the work to stay on the right path.

I think at first addiction is a choice. We choose to do things to numb the pain, to make us feel better. But, after it sucks you in, and you don't choose it. I think after sometime it becomes and illness that you just can't seem to get rid of.

8. What is the biggest thing you have lost from your loved ones addiction?

The biggest thing I have lost from addiction is my family. Addiction completely changed who we all used to be and has put wedges in all of our relationships, made us build walls up around our hearts and has caused a ton of resentment. It's going to be a long road ahead before things will ever be the same.

The biggest thing I have lost from addiction is my brother. I never lived a day without him. 21 years of love, laughs, fights, being raised by a single mom he helped raise me, he was a father figure, my protector, my role model, my friend. This addiction had taken everything that my family was, and torn it into pieces.

9. What do you think was the main reason they started using?

I think the main reason they started using was to numb the pain. When he lost his buddy over in Afghanistan, he just fell apart. He started drinking too much, over using pills, then when my family finally put their foot down, he went spiraling. He lost his job, he could no longer afford the pills, so heroin was a cheaper fix. He never dealt with his pain, he just got a temporary high to tuck it away in the back of his mind.

10. Do you ever wish you could trade places with them?

I would take his place in a heart beat. He had so much potential, so much life to live. He has a little boy, and he deserves his daddy. I wish I could have taken all his pain.

11. Do you wish now that you would have reached out more? Do you think it would have made a difference?

I believe that the individuals must want sobriety for themselves, there's nothing we can do for them, and in most cases being there for them only enables them.

I wish I would have made him feel like I understood. The last 7 months of his life I was so rude. I didn't want to spend time with him because he was always nodding out, all he wanted was to hangout, and instead I just pulled the tough love approach. Now, more than ever, I wish I could just watch a movie with him, give him a hug, let him know that I loved him despite this terrible habit that he had formed. Ultimately, I don't know if it would have made a difference, or if he still would be here today, but at least I would have happier memories with him for the last couple months of his life than I did.

Questions and responses from my own mother:

1. If you could change one thing about your sons' addiction what would it be?

Of course if I could change one thing about my sons addiction it would be for him to not have one. But, what I would change is how my son must feel about himself to put drugs into his body and destroy himself. Your mind runs all day wondering if your child is okay, or if you're going to get a call that he is gone. All you can think about is, is my child going to overdose, or is someone going to hurt him because of his lifestyle? You worry all day if he is hungry and you just feel completely helpless because you still think of him as a child, when he was so funny and so full of life. The hardest part is not letting it consume your life because you have other children who you love more than life itself.

2. Do you take it personal that your son uses?

I try not to take it personal. But, I do. As a mom you want the best for you children. I question myself where did I go wrong with him, what did I do different with him that I didn't do with my other kids. Did I not discipline him enough. It hurts me to my core every single day. But, I try to just keep it to myself as much as possible.

3. What is one thing you wish you could understand about addiction?

I wish I could help people love themselves and not turn to drugs because of not feeling worthy or good enough. I would like to understand why a person starts to use them in the first place. What makes them turn to that.

4. How has addiction affected your other kids' lives?

I feel like its affected them because its made them see things maybe others can't see because they have been so close it, that now because they have a brother who uses, they want to take their own pain by helping other people understand it better, they are both trying to change the way things are now.

5. How has addiction affected you personally?

It's made me have a better understanding of it. But, it has also given me a lot of sleepless nights worrying about my own child, while also making me more sympathetic towards others who fight it because I wasn't very sympathetic before my own child struggled with it.

6. Did you ever think being with an addict would ever affect your kids' choices later in life?

I thought that if I raised my kids away from their dad and kept them away from it as much as I could that they wouldn't want that lifestyle or ever have to see that lifestyle. But, it didn't happen that way, it wasn't that easy to just get rid of their pain.

7. Do you wish now that you never would have had a relationship with an addict?

That's a hard question because yes I wish things were different for my son, but all I can think is that hopefully addiction stops at him and doesn't get passed on to my grandson. I didn't think that the trait or desire could get passed on, so I never thought it would affect my own kids, but it has. I would never change being with their father though because then I wouldn't have the kids I have now.

8. Do you think you have played apart in someones addiction, if so how, and why?

Yes. I can admit that I enable my son and always have, and still do to this day no matter how bad he gets. I do it because I am afraid that he won't talk to me anymore if I don't and that something bad will happen to him, that if I don't help him he will rob someone or get in a lot more trouble.

9. Do you wish you would have done things differently for your child?

Yes, I wish I would have paid more attention to what my child was doing when he was younger. I wish I would have got him counseling for the problems he faced because after a certain age you can't force your kids to do anything anymore.

10. What is your worst fear that can come from addiction?

Obviously my worst fear is that my son will die and that I will get a phone call telling me my son is gone, and that I am powerless to it and have no control over helping him anymore.

Questions and answers from those who beat addiction:

Anonymous:

1. Why did you ever start using? Was there one specific reason?

I had just left my husband and my girls were at their grandma's house for the summer, so I ended up just getting around the wrong crowd. And when I was high, I felt like I was on top of the world.

I started using to make friends and to get away from home. I had just moved to Longview Washington and I desperately wanted to fit in, but re-invent myself as someone totally different from my previous home, so I started selling ecstasy at parties mainly just for the simple fact that the "thizz" man would always have an invite to ALL the parties.

2. What finally made you stop using?

I haven't stopped. I still use because I haven't found myself. I still don't know who I am and that's all I know. I don't know how to be comfortable in my own skin.

I went to prison for 5 years and came out to a whole new world. There are so many resources out here like suboxine (which I am on) to help struggling addicts.

My kids, and I had nothing left. I ended up in a shelter.

3. What was one thing you lost during your time of addiction you wish you could get back?

I have two older girls I lost when they were 11 and 13 and my oldest daughter won't talk to me. I have rebuilt a relationship with my other daughter and I managed to keep my other two kids all through my addiction.

I lost my chance to do good in school, to get ahead and maybe not be where I am today.

Mine and my ex girlfriends baby that was aborted because I was on drugs and young and immature and not prepared for life with another life counting on me.

4. What would you say now to people who don't use, to help them better understand addiction?

You may think drugs make you cool and help you "fit in" but in reality, you are driving a wedge into life between you and your actual loved ones.

It's never worth what you will lose. You are not invincible.

There was nothing anyone could say to me, I was going to stop on my own time and my time only. It didn't matter how sad someone got, I still used. It sucked.

5. Do you think your addiction has changed who you are today?

I can't really say, I don't know who I am still.

Yes and no. I feel like I am a stronger person for what I have been through, but I know I could have been better If I never would have used.

Absolutely! I am 27, but I have an old soul that has seen enough hard times for 10 peoples lives. I experienced it all, and I only have one major regret, which was aborting my child.

6. Do you think you will ever be the same as you were before the addiction?

Not a chance in hell, that cute little innocent boy is gone forever.

I never knew who I was.

7. When did you know you were an addict, was there one specific moment, or time?

2012 when I was in jail and got dope sick for the first time.

When I spent my food money on drugs and living in my truck with my kids.

8. **What was your happiest moment in your life? Did you lose it because of your addiction? Do you think you can ever get it back?**

High school, playing football, and as a matter of fact yes I am finally getting that back because I am clean now. I start playing semi pro football for the Washington Cavaliers in a couple of weeks.

I lost my happiness moment in life, that's why I turned to drugs in the first place so no, now I will definitely never get it back. He's gone forever.

9. **Was the high worth what you lost?**

On an overall basis, no it wasn't worth it. But, the ecstasy days were amazing and the high was worth every lost item. But, that was just the gateway to the shards and darkness that destroyed my life.

No. The high was not worth what I lost. I am so deeply hurt from all of what I caused there is so much I can not get back or give back. I hurt everyday for what I did to my older girls, I am ashamed of who I was when I was using.

10. **What keeps you from using again?**

Pure drive. Determination and disgust for the result of what drugs do to people.

My kids. They are number one and the reason I am where I am today, and who I am today.

I know I am better than who I was becoming, and that keeps me going.

11. **Do you wish someone would have reached out more during your
time of addiction? Do you think it would have made a difference
in your use?**

I had a lot of people reach out and try to help and the more they did, the more resentful I became of them because I thought I had it under control.

No; I wish I would have reached out more and been honest.

12. **Looking back during your time of addiction, was there one thing
or multiple things you would have done differently in regards to**

your loved ones trying to understand you better?

I regret not being vulnerable and transparent with my family and friends. It's very difficult to step up and open up that line of communication carrying all the guilt, shame and embarrassment inside. It's all fear based. I was fearful of the reactions I would receive from the people I loved and let down. Living the majority of my life as an athlete/ leader, it was tremendously difficult to humble myself and have that conversation about drug addiction. It shows weakness and I've been coached and taught through sports and life to never show weakness.

13. **What was one of the biggest things that addiction took from you mentally, physically and emotionally? Have you got it back since you have been clean? Do you think that you will or ever can get it back?**

- Mentally: My confidence
- Physically: Joint and muscle pain
- Emotionally: Self love/ compassion

Just like it took time to lose things, it takes time to regain them. The longer someone uses drugs for escape, the longer and harder it is to get acclimated to feelings. I used drugs everyday for 3 years and it took roughly the same amount of sober time to get everything I lost back. It does come back tenfold.

Questions and answers from those who currently use:
Anonymous

1. **Why did you ever start using? Was there any one specific reason?**
At first there wasn't any real reason, I was just young. I Started with pot and alcohol and just thought what I was doing was cool and was experimenting and that nothing would ever come from it, we were just kids and I thought our parents would take care of everything. And then it just escalated, as I got older, I had surgery and was prescribed pain pills by the doctor and that's where

it all started, I loved the feeling they gave me and didn't know what would come from it. After that, it just became normal to get high.

2. Do you blame others for your use?

I used to blame my father, but as I've gotten older I've realized that I just have an addiction problem and there's no one else to blame but myself now.

3. What's the scariest thing that's happened to you while you have used?

This is sort of a day by day thing now. Crazy shit happens to me all the time. It's just became a normal part of my lifestyle now. But recently, I went out to meet my drug connect and was in the car with the person and they decided to drop me off in the pitch black along the river with no cell phone service, and said they would be back to pick me up, and I thought I was going to be killed, luckily I wasn't. But, I felt like I was. Another thing would be getting a gun pulled on me and being threatened to give up my drugs or I would be shot. This is something that happens to people who are addicts all the time, it happened to my buddy, someone broke into their house and zip tied their family and said if they didn't tell them where the money and drugs were they would be killed, addicts in my circle do this often because they are so desperate.

4. Who do you think you have hurt the most during your time of addiction?

Myself because I was living a good life, had everything going for me with sports and had a basketball scholarship to college. But, then I gave it all up to heroin because I didn't love myself enough to quit and try and live a better life. Now, here I am 10 years later still living this lifestyle.

5. Do you think drugs have affected you more physically or mentally, or both?

Both, because I have used for 12 years, I might possibly have hep C now and mrsa and all the other things that can come from drug use, but I'm too afraid to go to the doctor. And my brain from using so many drugs has made me so paranoid and has made me do and say thing to people I never would have imagined saying while I was sober.

6. How has being around other addicts affected your own influence on drug addiction?

The more people you are around that use, the more you want to use. If you are are alone, you dont use as much because it's just you. You do things that put you more at risk when you're around others, you put yourself in a bad environment and in situations where you can't trust anyone around you. When you live this lifestyle you're constantly around people who smile in your face, but who are actually trying to do things to harm you. And, It's harder to say no when you are around other people who are using because it's just more of a trigger for you.

7. How has your drug addiction affected your loved ones?

I've put them through hell because they aren't able to see what type of person I can be when I'm clean and sober. I'm loving and caring and am a good person who wouldn't do some of these things I would do when I'm high, that everyday regular people aren't used to seeing- like stealing my grandmas purse and her car to get drugs and stealing my moms' purse and being chased by my family down the street all because I wanted to get high. The worst part is, they can see the seriousness of the situation of what I was doing, but I couldn't. I just was desperate. They try to help all they can and it breaks their and my heart because there's only so much they can do. It's kept me away from my kids who don't deserve that and they don't know why I'm not around and its affected them by not having me around. I've lost a lot of my families trust, and it just becomes a cycle because I always say I'm gonna do something different next time, and never do. I just end up relapsing over and over, and it's hard to gain anyone's trust back this way.

8. Do you think you have played a part in someone else's addiction?

Iv'e never really been the type to influence those who are clean to use again, but I've sold drugs, so I have contributed to getting people high and potentially ruining their lives just to benefit me, instead of helping people to stay clean. I've been lonely and have asked people to use with me just to have someone around but I've never felt like I needed to get others high, I just dont feel good about myself.

9. Is the high worth what you have lost?

Not at all, the high is great, but now I try and chase it everyday, but it's no where near worth who I've hurt. I've lost friendships, family, trust and my kids.

10. Do you think you will ever be the same after all this even if you get clean?

Definitely not because I will always know all the things I've done and been through, and, I'll always remember that. It always reminds me how low I've been. It's something I will have to deal with it the rest of my life, I'll know that I am not like everyone else. I can't just have a drink or try it one more time because an addict cant do that, because 1 time leads to 2 years down the road and you're still using.

11. Do you think you will ever stop, if so what's it going to take?

Ya I think that I 100 percent am going to stop. I don't know what it will take or when, hopefully it takes being so sick and tired of it and this lifestyle that I just quit. It's gonna lead to jail or death and I know that and realize that. I know that I have to love myself more, and that I have to love and be there for my kids because my dad wasn't around and now I know that it affects kids so much when someone isn't in their lives, so being around my own kids is a huge motivation for me. Also, I think that an ultimatum would help me stop. My family telling me I either stop, or that they won't be able to be apart of my life anymore.

12. If you could help others understand addiction better, what would you tell them?

If it was younger kids, who might start drinking or smoking, I would say ya it does seem fun in the beginning and every thing is carefree, but to tell them to look what it can really do to a person. I would tell them that I thought it was fun too, but now 10 years later I have nothing and never imagined it would get this far. It's not something anyone ever wants to go through. Drugs tear everything apart- your families, your friendships, you. It becomes a disease that you don't know how to cure. I would say how important it is to have a good support system because it's hard to do it on your own. All that it will lead too if you do become an addict, and use drugs is addiction, jail or death. Thats all it leads to. There's no way around it. If you can't get out of it, that's the only result. And, even if you do get clean, it'll be apart of your life forever; it will never go away. You have to learn your triggers and your memories and understand that you're not like everyone else because some people can drink one time or use one time, and never again, but addicts aren't like everyone else.

As you can see, you are not alone in this battle. So many people today are negatively affected by this epidemic, but sadly, not enough people are taught how to actually cope with it. Learning ways to confront and address all problems within this war will not only help you live a happier and more stress free life, but it will also allow you to look deeper into addiction, learn new perspectives, and prepare yourself better within your own child's, friends, or loved ones' fight with addiction.

Chapter 15: You Are the Answer

As I'm sitting here trying to write my last chapter, my mom called me to tell me my brother has been arrested with a new charge — possession and selling of narcotics. As many times as I've gotten the call that my brother was going back to jail, this time it was different. Usually I just say "oh okay how long do you think he will get?" But, this time I could hear the seriousness in her shaking voice. I felt sick to my stomach because I knew it was real, and that he would face more consequences. The crazy thing is I just sat down and talked to him 2 days before this. 2 days!! Now I might not see my brother for a really long time. That's the reality though, you never know what's going to happen being apart of this lifestyle, it's a day to day struggle no matter who you are!

As much as I try to help others cope with their loved ones addiction, it still is always going to hurt me to my core to know my brother is an addict, and that I can't physically and mentally help him. He sat there with me at dinner days before he went to jail and he said to me there is no other way out of addiction, it's either jail or death.

JAIL or DEATH. These two words came out of his mouth like they meant nothing to him - like he was saying love and happiness. But, at the end of the day, he still left and chose that life, knowing his only two consequences. They all do. We cannot change them, we cannot make them stop, and we cannot force them to get clean. The only power and responsibility we hold in this war, is OUR OWN.

No matter how much love and support you give your children, your friends, your mom, your brother or your significant other, they are still human beings and you are NOT their only influence. You are not the reason they continue to use, they will not stop for you, they are not doing this to hurt you, and they will not change until they are ready to change on their own.

As you can see, the battle never really ends, even for someone like me, someone who has learned every coping mechanism there is to try and be okay with this way of living. I am still human. I still get sad, and I still will always care for my loved ones who have an addiction problem. That will never change. What is different from before, is now I am capable of being OKAY with MYSELF and my own feelings of how I view addiction, allowing me to take a step back, and continue to love my brother and other family members no matter what happens because life is way too short not to, especially that kind of life.

I was once just like you, stuck, scared, confused, hurt, betrayed, lost. Always asking myself why and how my loved ones could continue to live such a disastrous lifestyle. Searching for answers that couldn't be answered. I was hateful. I was resentful. I hated drugs. I hated everything that was associated with them and thought the people who used them just made excuses. Believe me, you are not the only one who feels or felt this way. It took me years and countless mistakes to learn how to understand and cope with this lifestyle. It took hurtful words towards people I care about, hateful actions, and losing someone to finally wake me up. I wish I could take it all back everyday.

Understanding drug addiction is no longer about hope. It's not about faith. Those 2 things will not help you anymore. It's about the truth. And the truth is, your son, your daughter, your friend or whoever you love is an addict and always will be, even after they are clean. The only person you can fully take responsibility for in this world is yourself. You have to learn how to be in control of your own mind and take action into your own hands when it comes to learning to cope with what has been placed into your life forever, because this will be a life long battle for everyone involved. Addiction will be a constant struggle day in and day out. You cannot win the war against drug addiction as a user, or as a loved one, if you cannot win the war against your own mind. YOU, and only YOU have the responsibility for your own life and YOUR own happiness. No matter how far off your loved one has traveled in the wrong direction, it is their responsibility to find their way back, and to find a new path. It is never too late, and it is never too late for you as an outsider to take back your own life in the mean time. Choosing to change your own perspective on this lifestyle is left completely up to you. Just remember, you don't have to feel this way anymore, you don't have to be miserable. You are stronger than you think. You don't have to be stuck like I was. You are capable of turning your own life around by taking action into your own hands. Addiction does not have to consume your entire life, UNLESS YOU allow it to! Be the own change in your life that you are longing for. Be your own answer. YOU ARE the answer you have been searching for.

I went above and beyond to try and understand this lifestyle. I was so desperate to get my life back that I really thought trying to become a temporary user would give me the answers. Thankfully, my days are looking brighter since my experiment, and I am beginning to feel the effects from the pills less and less each day.

I am 26 years old. My father, brother, cousin, grandma, grandpa and great uncle and aunt still continue to use to this day. I cannot change this no matter how hard I try. I cannot change them. This is their life until they WANT to stop. If they ever do. Their life is NOT my life anymore. I hope I've made it clear that the only thing I can do, and the only thing you can do for your loved ones in this lifelong battle is to love them for who they are, pray for them, stop making excuses, and take your own life back into your hands. IT'S TIME!